THE
COVENT GARDEN
COOKBOOK

MARIE STONE

Allison and Busby Limited London

First published in Great Britain by
Allison and Busby Limited
6a Noel Street London W1V 3RB

© Marie Stone 1974

Reprinted 1979

Printed and bound by
The Pitman Press, Bath

ACKNOWLEDGEMENTS

My most grateful thanks are extended to the following, without whose generous cooperation this book would have been impossible: Jasper Tomlinson, Graham Snow, Keith Robinson, Christie Wyld, Alison Latey, Susie Davies, Carol Eisler, Jennifer Button, Philip Ward-Jackson, Michelle Hanson, Brian Anson, John McGleash, Michael and Jennifer Graham-Jones, Basil Bell, Tahera Jilani, Jane Randell, Sally Hill, Lesley Watters and John Gage; to Aean Pinheiro for the design of this book and to David Shaply of *The Fruit Trades Journal* for kind permission to reproduce the fruit and vegetable supply calendar; to the staffs of the London Library, the British Museum, the Westminster Library, the County Hall Prints Library, the Science Museum, the Radio Times Hulton Picture Library, the British Film Institute, the Royal Photographic Society, the Covent Garden Market Authority, the Guildhall Library, the Mushroom Growers' Association, the British Farm Produce Council, the Royal Horticultural Society Library, and the Covent Garden Community Association; to the many others who have helped me with recipes or with information about Covent Garden, many of whom are mentioned in the text; and above all to the people in the market who, because of their notable directness, clarity and humour, made this book a pleasure to write.

CONTENTS

STORIES FROM COVENT GARDEN

LIST OF ILLUSTRATIONS

Throughout this book the pictures of vegetables are taken from the Robinson edition of Vilmorin-Andrieux's *Vegetable Garden* (London, 1905) and the pictures of fruit are taken from Charles Baltet's *Traite de la Culture Fruitere Commerciale et Bourgeoise* (Paris, 1908).

INTRODUCTION

Covent Garden, with its famous market for fruit, vegetables and flowers, has been an attraction for Londoners and visitors alike for over three hundred years.

Originally the garden of a Westminster convent the district became, with the encouragement of Charles I, London's smartest residential square and subsequently the site of two of the great theatres established by Charles II. By Hogarth's day Covent Garden had fallen from grace but was still magnetic: the heartland of night-life and dissipation. The market, however, thrived. The local theatres too multiplied, until now nearly half the theatres of London, as well as the national opera and ballet companies, can be found there. The atmosphere of creativity, the historical and romantic associations of the old buildings, the variety of restaurants and pubs combined with the irrepressible energy of the market itself, have made Covent Garden one of the liveliest and most versatile parts of the capital. But by 1974 a decision had been irrevocably taken to move the market abruptly to a new and less attractive location some miles away, leaving a problem area for planners, property developers, politicians and people, together with many memories.

Although this is first and foremost a cookery book, I wanted it to reflect all the many aspects of the place and so some of the memories, the history and, indeed, some of the problems have also been included. The historical descriptions appear throughout the book in italics and in roughly chronological order, just as the food has been arranged in more or less the order of a meal: the early days of the convent garden and the soup recipes come near the beginning, and so on through the book, until with the desserts and beverages we reach the present day.

Vegetarianism is not the subject of this book. If you incline towards it, as I often do, you need to know a lot about cereals and protein-rich foods of vegetable origin that is not really within the scope of the Covent Garden Market. Fruit and vegetables are the main ingredients of most of the recipes, and though the book does not aim to be encyclopaedic I hope it is found complete enough for practical use. Wherever possible I have given characteristic recipes for each item, so that for many English vegetables recipes from traditional local sources are given as well as cooking tips from my own experience, whereas for the more exotic items that appear in the market I have used many recipes from abroad.

The ingredients in the recipes, unless otherwise indicated, are in quantities about sufficient for four people, so that the arithmetic involved in decreasing or increasing the numbers will be fairly simple. Within each subject grouping (for example "Soup" or "Vegetables" or "Fruit") the order is alphabetical, and wherever a recipe assumes some knowledge of another recipe, such as for a particular sauce, you will be able to find it under the appropriate heading. The index, of course, can also be referred to in case of difficulty. To avoid repeating the same instructions again and again, I have given only a few examples of such basic processes as steaming vegetables and stewing fruit, which are obviously very widely applicable.

I hope that this book is useful for its information about food and will help more than occasionally towards a really good meal. Having briefly but intensely been involved in the affairs of this very interesting place in the centre of London, and living as a near neighbour, I also hope the book will encourage involvement with all our surroundings, wherever we happen to be living or working.

Kitchen Equipment

It should be noted that it is worth buying the best equipment you can afford; not only will this make cooking more enjoyable and convenient but it may also in the long run prove to be a saving.

Every cooking operation is easier with good heavy saucepans, cast-iron frying pans and the appropriate sized dishes.

Sharp knives are more easily controlled than blunt ones and are therefore safer. I have never found anything better than a steel for sharpening, but stainless knives may need a special quality sharpening steel.

I use a Moulinex liquidizer of the continental type. This is on a stalk and can be used in any container, including a saucepan on the stove. Any quantity can be liquidized at one time and cleaning is no problem.

Temperature and Timing

Cooking times are of course approximate. With vegetables they depend on season, age and individual taste. (For three hundred years cookery books have pointed out that the English overcook their vegetables.) The following table shows the oven settings that apply throughout the book:

Gas	Fahrenheit	Centigrade	Description
½	250	121	very slow/very low
1	275	135	very slow/very low
2	300	149	slow/low
3	325	163	warm
4	350	177	moderate/medium
5	375	190	moderately hot
6	400	205	moderately hot
7	425	218	hot
8	450	232	very hot
9	475	246	very hot

Weights and Measures

"The dangerous person in the kitchen is the one who goes rigidly by weights, measurements, thermometers and scales. I would say once more that all these scientific implements are not of much use, the only exception being for making pastry and jams, where exact weights are important"—Marcel Boulestin, *What Shall We Have Today?* (1931).

I agree that exact quantities are usually unnecessary but find that even the most experienced cooks feel more secure with at least an approximate guide. With metrication, weights and measures are on their way to becoming simpler to understand although in the kitchen a kilogram may seem too large a unit and a gramme too small. The following conversion tables may be some help:

Weights
1 ounce = 28.35 grammes
1 pound (16 oz) = 454 grammes
Therefore 100 grammes roughly equal 3½ oz, and ½ kilogram is roughly 10% more than 1 lb.

Capacities
1 imperial pint = 0.568 litres
1 imperial gallon (8 pints) = 4.546 litres
Therefore 1 litre is about 10% less than a quart (2 pints).
10 millilitres (1% of a litre) is roughly equal to 1/3 fluid oz = 1 dessertspoon.

It is useful to know that one Imperial gallon of water weights 10 lbs (160 oz) and equals 10 US pints. A cup in either US or British measure is a ½ pint.

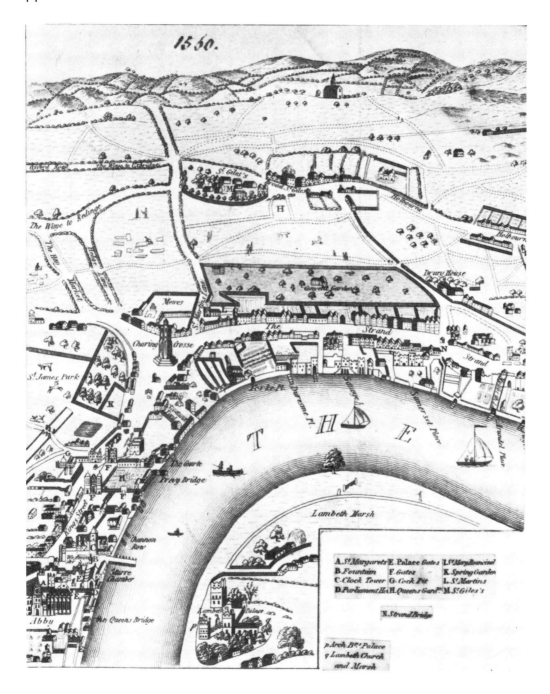

1560.

The Wave to Redinge

St Giles's

Holbourn

Holbourne

The Wave to Redinge

Drury House

Covent Garden

Mewes

Charing Crosse

The Strand

Strand

St James Park

K

N

T H E

The Courte
Privy Bridge

Lambeth Marsh

G
F
F
F

Kings Street

Channon Row

Westm:
the hall

Starre
Chamber

Abby

The Queens Bridge

Lambeth Palace

A. St Margarets   E. Palace Gates   I. St Mary Honcind
B. Fountain   F. Gates   K. Spring Garden
C. Clock Tower   G. Cock Pit   L. St Martins
D. Parliament Ho: H. Queens Gard: M. St Giles's

N. Strand Bridge

p Arch: Bps Palace
q Lambeth Church
and Marsh

Right: newspaper cutting of 1739 about the early history of the area

Left: map of central London showing the "Convent" Garden, 1560

The PARISH of St. PAUL's Covent-Garden.

1739

THE Ground on which this Parish is built, was formerly Fields, with some thatched Houses, Stables, and such like, which lying in so good a Place, the Owner of the said Ground, the then Earl of *Bedford*, thought good to make an Improvement thereof, and procuring an Act of Parliament for making it into a Parish of it self, disunited from St. *Martin's in the Fields*, did, about the Years 1634 and 1635, begin to pull down the said old Buildings, and clear away the Rubbish, and laid it out into several fair Streets, streight and uniform, which were built with good Brick Buildings. About the Centre of the Ground he caused to be set out a large Square, or rather oblong Piece of Ground, 500 Feet in Length, and 400 in Breadth; and into this Plat of Ground four large Streets at first had their Entrance; but now there are five, of 50 or 60 Feet broad, *viz. Ruffel-ftreet* on the East, *James-ftreet* on the North, *King-ftreet* and *Henrietta-ftreet* on the West, and *South-hampton-ftreet* on the South, which was last built, with other Places adjoining, on the Ground where *Bedford* House and Gardens stood. On the North and East Sides of this Square are erected stately Buildings for the Dwellings of Persons of Fashion, their Fronts standing on Pillars and Arches of Brick and Stone Rustick Work, with Piazza's or Walks like those in the *Royal-Exchange* in LONDON, and imitating the *Rialto* in *Venice*. At the North East Angle of these Piazza's is the Entrance into the New Theatre, lately erected, the Frontispiece of which is a very expensive Piece of Work, but highly condemned by good Architects, as full of Absurdities. Since the first Building, this Parish has had great Improvements, as well by its Houses as its Inhabitants.

AND if we consider this Parish, as to its fine, streight, and broad Streets, replenished with good Buildings, and so well inhabited by a Mixture of Nobility, Gentry, and wealthy Tradesmen, here seated since the Fire of LONDON, 1666, scarce admitting of any Poor, not being pestered with mean Courts and Alleys; likewise its open and large Piazza or Garden, so delightful to walk in: It may deserve to be accounted one of the best Parishes in the City of LONDON, *Weftminfter*, and the Parts adjacent. This Parish is begirted on all Sides by St. *Mar-tin's in the Fields*, out of which it was taken.

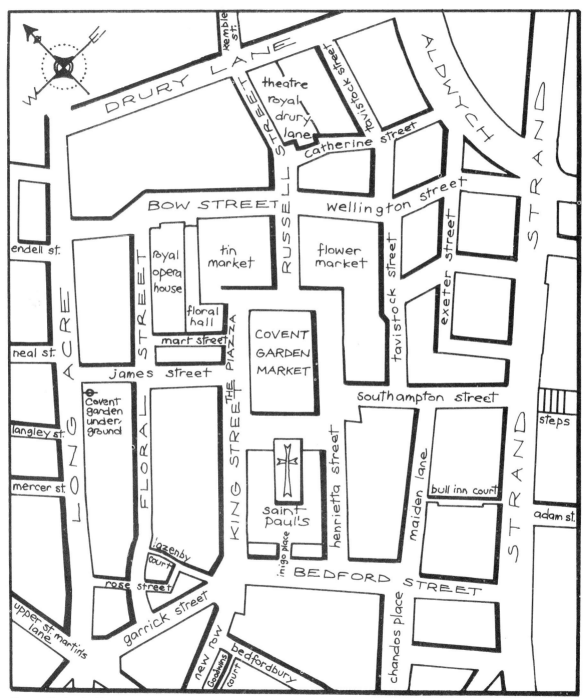

Covent Garden in 1974

SAUCES, BATTERS, PASTRY

If you doubt your ability to boil an egg, you are by definition someone who cannot cook. To hesitate before performing a miracle is a natural thing to do, though, if you think about it. It is just that a boiled egg is so commonplace that its strangeness is taken for granted. If cookery were thought of as a science instead of an art, then sauces would be interesting demonstrations of colloidal suspensions and emulsions, of osmosis through semi-permeable membranes, of the chemical cross-linking between molecular chains. They are, however, basic to the art of cookery; the nuts and bolts that hold it together.

Since this is not a cookery encyclopaedia, three things only are attempted here. First, to give instructions for preparations which recur throughout the book, such as Béchamel sauce or shortcrust pastry. Secondly, to draw attention to some of the miracles: if you heat a tomato enough you expect to get first a cooked tomato and finally a burnt tomato — that is ordinary experience — but mayonnaise, Béchamel, even boiled cornflour are something quite different, something quite new and unpredictable wrought from eggs and oil, flour, butter and milk. Thirdly, a few of the more common preparations from French cookery are given yet again some definition which may be of help.

One of the basic basics is a *roux*. This is simply butter and flour, in roughly equal quantities, heated together whilst stirring continuously. The greater the heat, the more you cook the flour and the darker it gets. If you then moisten with water, stock, milk or wine, you get a thickening that may be used for soups, stews or as a basic sauce to pour over something. Another more delicate way to thicken a stew is with *beurre manié*, which is a lump, or lumps, of butter about the size of pebbles rolled, or squashed, into flour. A further, very unclassical, way to thicken with starch is to mix flour (or cornflour) and water to a thin cream and add the mixture to any hot liquid that requires thickening. This method is most successful if it is done in stages, bringing the liquid to boil in between to see how much more thickening is required.

Other methods of thickening hot sauces are with egg yolk, which is beaten and added to the hot liquid (not too hot or it will curdle) and then gently heated while stirring continuously, or by thickening with cream. The latter is very tricky as you may have to use so much to achieve anything that the result is both a financial and a health disaster, so it is best to experiment with this technique on a small scale until practice makes perfect.

A general hint is to remember to taste everything before turning it out of the saucepan. Some quite ordinary things, such as vinegar, cider, Worcestershire sauce, a clove, even freshly-ground black pepper, can effect surprising transformations if a little extra touch is needed.

Aspic

Aspic is meat jelly. It derives its name from one of the herbs originally used to flavour it. You can make it by simmering a calf's foot with some other meat trimmings, onion, carrot, garlic and herbs. Then reduce until, on cooling, a jelly is obtained. A quick method is to use a good tablespoon of gelatine with two cupfuls of meat stock, soak the gelatine and then add to the hot stock and stir until dissolved, flavour with lemon juice or sherry. Aspic can be used to make something out of nothing if the nothing includes ends of chicken, seafood, vegetables, hardboiled eggs and maybe some fresh herbs. To clarify aspic, briskly heat to boiling point while whisking in egg white complete with shell, the shell crunched up. Simmer for ten minutes then strain through a fine sieve.

Apple Sauce

This is an essentially sharp sauce to eat with rich food like pork, duck or goose. Peel, core and slice 1 lb of cooking apples, and put them to sweat over a gentle heat with ½ oz of butter, stirring occasionally until they disintegrate to a pulp and can be stirred into a smooth creamy purée. Moisten with a little water if they stick or become too dry.

Béchamel Sauce

This creamy white sauce is said to have been introduced by Béchamel, the Marquis of Nointel, Lord Steward of Louis XIV's Household.

The exact quantities for four people are ¾ oz butter, ¾ oz flour and ½ pint milk.

Gently melt butter and stir in an equal amount of plain flour. When the mixture begins to bubble stir in hot milk, a little at a time. Season to taste with pepper, salt and nutmeg; the milk could have been improved by boiling an onion in it. After cooling off a little the sauce can be enriched if you like, by adding beaten egg yolk.

Some of the variations of Béchamel are:

Mornay Sauce – add grated cheese, preferably Parmesan, to hot Béchamel.

Marinière Sauce – make the Béchamel with stock instead of milk, remove from the heat, stir in cream equal in amount to the butter used, followed by beaten egg yolk, then add finely chopped shallots and parsley. This is a very good sauce for freshly cooked mussels, if you are lucky enough to have some.

Poulette Sauce – this is made in the same way as Marinière sauce but is seasoned with herbs instead of shallots and parsley.

Sauce Bourguignonne

Put some chopped bacon in a heavy saucepan and cover with chopped carrots and onions and a bayleaf and some thyme. Sweat these over a low heat and then add wine, pepper and minced garlic. Cook gently until brown, thick and sticky then add some stock or bouillon. The sauce can be liquidized or pushed through a sieve.

Custard

Heat ¾ pint milk to just below boiling point, put 3 oz sugar into it and stir with a vanilla pod, or add ½ teaspoon of vanilla extract. Beat up 2 eggs in a bowl and gradually add the mixture to them, stirring all the time. Stand the bowl above a saucepan of gently boiling water and continue stirring until the custard thickens to the consistency of heavy cream.

Sauce Espagnole or Brown Sauce

Slice an onion and a carrot and simmer in a covered heavy saucepan with some scraps of lean white meat, preferably veal or ham, and a clove. When a sort of brown gravy is obtained work in a dessertspoonful of plain flour, moisten with some bouillon and keep hot, cooking very slowly for several hours, until a consistency of thick cream is obtained. The sauce may then be liquidized or pushed through a sieve.

Sauce Hollandaise

This sauce is made without flour and is a sort of hot mayonnaise.
   Warm and melt 4 oz of butter in a double saucepan. Mix in the beaten yolks of three eggs and stir. While it is thickening put in a further 4 oz of butter piece by piece, stirring gently all the time. When thickened, the sauce may be seasoned with salt and pepper and some vinegar or lemon juice may be added.

Maltaise Sauce

This is a fragrant variation of Hollandaise. Add orange juice, preferably from a blood orange, and shavings of the rind to a hot Hollandaise.

Mousseline Sauce

This is fifty-fifty Hollandaise and stiffly whipped cream. Best performed in the double saucepan, folding the cream in whilst keeping warm. Adjust seasoning after adding cream.

Oxford Sauce or Cumberland Sauce

To make a port and orange sauce use equal quantities of port, redcurrant jelly and orange and lemon juice mixed, seasoned with Worcestershire sauce and mustard. For Oxford sauce shavings of orange peel cut in strips are blanched in the hot wine, while for Cumberland sauce glacé cherries are added to the sauce before serving. Rich food such as duck or baked ham may benefit by being served with this sharp, peppery, fruity sauce.

Either proceed by reducing the wine by boiling sufficiently so that when mixed with the fruit juices and molten redcurrant jelly, a sauce of the right consistency is obtained or make it by thickening the wine by boiling with a little cornflour until it is quite thick and syrupy before mixing with the fruit juices and molten redcurrant jelly.

Sweet and Sour Sauce

Stir a tablespoonful of flour into an equal amount of melted butter and heat until golden brown. Add a cupful of vegetable water or stock and a tablespoonful of vinegar and one of sugar, beat well until smooth and season with salt, pepper and some French mustard. The Chinese sweet and sour sauce is translucent and being made without fat or oil is lighter and more of a favourite with slightly undercooked and crunchy vegetables. Since the Chinese version is usually best made in with the vegetables themselves and not separately there is no precise recipe. To the cooking juices vinegar, soy sauce and sugar or honey are added in roughly equal volumes and thickened with corn or potato starch. A pinch of powdered ginger may be included.

Tomato Sauce

Cook together with oil for about 20 minutes 2 lbs of ripe tomatoes, an onion, a carrot, some celery, some parsley, all finely chopped. This makes a good sauce for spaghetti, rice, fried chicken and all manner of fried vegetables and rissoles. Season with salt, pepper and a little sugar. Basil, especially fresh basil, is a great improver. If you want the sauce smooth, liquidize or push it through a sieve.

Mayonnaise

The old and difficult method of making this miraculous stuff is to put egg yolk, free of white, into a basin and add olive oil, drop by drop, stirring all the time with a wooden spoon. When it becomes thick, creamy and golden, flavour with vinegar or lemon juice, pepper, salt and some mustard, if you like mustard. If, in the making, it becomes too thick add the vinegar then, and if it does not work at all start again with a fresh lot of egg yolk, adding the unsuccessful mixture instead of the oil. Cool ingredients and tools increase the certainty of success.

The same basic idea with a liquidizer instead of a wooden spoon is a lot easier. A lighter mayonnaise is then possible using the whole egg, white and all.

Vinaigrette

Salads in summer bring the expectation of oil and vinegar. Vinaigrette is the two mixed with some seasoning.

"Three times the spoon with oil of Lucca crown,
And once with vinegar procured from Town."

A convenient procedure is to measure out the vinegar or lemon juice, add a little sugar, salt, pepper, mustard and herbs to your taste and then add about three times the volume of oil and stir vigorously.

Batter for Frying

Flour bound with egg forms a coating which, when dipped in hot oil, prevents the oil from soaking in and spoiling a delicate flavour. In general, sufficient whole egg is added to the flour to make a stiff paste and that is thinned out to the consistency of cream by stirring in milk or water. The batter may improve if it is left to stand for an hour or two. A little salt will improve the taste, especially if the batter is used for pancakes. The flour may be plain white flour but wholemeal or buckwheat flour may be used in varying proportions.

To make a batter for frying fruit, use 1 egg, 3 oz flour, ¼ pint of milk and a pinch of salt.

For vegetables, use 4 oz flour, 3 tablespoons olive oil and a pinch of salt; stir these together, adding a small cupful of tepid water until a smooth cream is obtained. Before use, stir in the stiffly-beaten white of an egg.

Caramel Sauce

Caramel is partly oxidized, that is to say burnt, sugar. If the caramel is to be any good at all the sugar must caramelize equally, just burning a bit of the sugar may give the right colour but will not give the right taste. Put 3 tablespoons of white sugar into a plain saucepan (plastic handles may get scorched) and moisten the sugar with just sufficient water so that when heated a clear, colourless syrup is formed. Boil the water off this syrup and when the water is gone the molten sugar gets hotter and hotter. It will then turn colour from straw to dark brown and it may froth up in the pan. At this stage, it will continue to bubble even off the heat — it is, in fact, burning but without a flame. When it is coffee-coloured the time has come to quench it by pouring it into about ½ pint of water which should be made ready beforehand. The quenching may fill the kitchen with steam and should be done in the bottom of the sink, at arms length and with the eyes averted to avoid being splashed by molten sugar. The results are usually worthwhile even if the method seems troublesome. The quenched caramel is then brought to the boil in order to dissolve it and then thickened to a syrup with a dessertspoonful of cornflour mixed with a little water, added bit by bit while the caramel is off the boil. A clove or a pinch of cinnamon may be added.

Chocolate Sauce

4 oz of plain chocolate are melted in a saucepan over a gentle heat together with a little butter to prevent the chocolate sticking. Add a cupful of milk and bring nearly to the boil, stirring frequently. Remove from the heat and stir in the beaten yolks of three or four eggs. You may need to heat the sauce gently, stirring continuously, in order to thicken it to the desired consistency.

An alternative, much plainer sauce, is made with cocoa, sugar, vanilla and water thickened with cornflour. A teaspoonful of coffee powder added makes the chocolate sauce into a *Mocha* sauce.

Fennel Sauce

Chop some fennel and blanch it by boiling it in salted water for a few minutes. Add the fennel to melted butter with some salt and pepper and serve with fish or chicken.

Short Crust Pastry

The main ingredients are flour, butter, salt and water but the flour used can be partly or wholly wholemeal, and margarine or some other shortening can be used instead of butter, and white wine, cider, milk or what have you instead of water. The salt of course has to be salt. Rub the shortening into the flour very lightly, with your fingertips. The shortest pastry would need about 10 oz of shortening for each pound of flour at the most, and anything less than 6 oz would give a rather doughy pastry. You can use as much as a teaspoon of salt per lb of flour. When rubbed in evenly add water, a bit at a time. Use about a cupful per lb of flour. Cut the dough continuously with a knife to mix in the water. You can add a whole egg instead of some of the water if you want a richer pastry. You have added enough water when the dough sticks together. Then put it aside in a cool place for some time, say, half an hour, before rolling it out.

The mixture of flour and water if worked or kneaded forms a stronger dough, tougher and more resistant to being torn than if it has not been worked. The aim with pastry is to keep it cool and not to work it at all, so that the result when cooked is not tough at all, but brittle, and light to eat. Bread dough, on the other hand, is deliberately worked to produce a stronger, tougher dough.

When the pastry is rolled out flat, using several dustings of flour to prevent sticking, roll it up on the rolling-pin in order to pick it up. You can then unroll it wherever you want, onto the top of a pie or onto a tray. This is a good tip, especially if your uncooked pastry is very tender, and tears easily, which is, of course, how it should be.

The exact quantities for four people, in order to cover or line an 8-inch pie dish, are ¼ lb flour, ¼ teaspoon salt, 2 oz butter and 2 tablespoons water. This makes 6 oz of pastry.

Sponge Mixture

Use a mixing bowl that fits into a saucepan of hot water. Whisk together eggs and sugar, an ounce of sugar for each egg. As it warms the mixture will thicken until it holds the marks of the whisk. Fold in an ounce of plain white flour for each egg, a clean hand being the most serviceable implement. Use the mixture immediately. A three-egg mixture is about right for a six-inch sponge cake. Cooking time is usually about 10 minutes, when the sponge will be golden, springy to the touch and a knife thrust in the centre comes out dry.

THE COVENT GARDEN PIAZZA

These portico buildings were designed to attract "Persons of great Distinction". The first residents included three Earls, and many other persons of title. Most of these early residents, mainly with Royalist sympathies, left the square during the second half of the 17th century. At this time Sir Peter Lely (1618-1680), Sir Godfrey Kneller (1646-1723) and other Stuart portrait painters and artists moved in. Lord Archer stayed in his house, visible in the top left-hand corner of the square, and existing today, until 1756. By then, William Maitland was to comment sadly that the Market had "proved so prejudicial to the Magnificent Buildings that instead of their being inhabited by Persons of the Greatest Distinction as formerly, they are now obliged to take up with Vinters, Coffeemen and such other inhabitants".

The market, established in 1670, moved into the square in 1705. The Piazza was losing some of its charm. The fashionable world was attracted west to new locations: Soho, St James and Leicester Squares.

Inigo Jones, the most important figure of English 17th-century art, had seen the chance of creating, on the Duke of Bedford's undeveloped estate, an Italian Piazza. It was a vision that had a brilliant but brief success. By its light, however, he enabled others to see the possibilities; he changed the shape of English town architecture.

Left: the Piazza, 1717

Above: Lord Archer's house, 43 King Street, 1754

SOUPS

"When you make any kind of soup, particularly vermicelli, portable or brown gravy soups, or any other soups that have herbs or roots in them, be sure to remember to lay your meat at the bottom of the pan, with a large piece of butter. Then cut the roots and herbs small, and having laid them over your meat, cover your pot or saucepan very close, and keep under it a slow fire, which will draw all the virtues out of the vegetables, turn them to a good gravy, and give the soup a very different flavour from what it would have by a contrary conduct." — John Farley, *The London Art of Cookery*, Published in Dublin, 1783.

"When you make any kind of soups more especially, portable, vermicelli, or brown gravy soup, or indeed any other that has roots or herbs in it, always observe to lay the meat at the bottom of your pan, with a good lump of butter. Cut the herbs and roots small, lay them over the meat, cover it close, and set it over a slow fire: this will draw all the virtue out of the roots or herbs, turn it to a good gravy, and give the soup a different flavour from what it would have on putting the water in at first." — William Augustus Henderson, *Housekeeper's instructor*, or *Universal Family Cook*, published in London, 1793

Any cookery book will have echoes of plagiarism; you will find the same vegetable served with the identical sauce, and so it should be. Elizabeth David discussing soups in her excellent *French Provincial Cooking*, devotes over two pages to advocating traditional wisdom and the use of recipes because what may be fun by the way of improvisation for the cooks "may induce a mood of gloomy apprehension in their families and guests". At the same time, it is probably true to say that if you wandered through Covent Garden in the middle of the morning, as some nuns do, carrying a bag into which you popped any discarded vegetables and you then chopped, boiled and liquidized the lot, added salt and pepper and a sprinkling of parsley you would have quite a tasty soup.

Many cooks warn against one particular hazard in soup making: avoid disguising the right taste of your chosen soup in the belief that stock is an essential ingredient. Plain water is often the only thing to use. This is a view stated strongly by Marcel Boulestin in his writings, and was supported by Mr. Gonzales, the very able chef of the Neal Street Restaurant.

The arrangement of the following soup recipes is rather random. The usual recommendations for preparing stock, the traditional *pot du feu* and so forth are omitted, as today the recipes are more easily come by than the ingredients and anyway stock cubes can usually be used as a substitute. It is interesting to note that "Portable soup" mentioned in the quotation is made from cutting up "three large legs of veal, one of beef and the lean part of a ham. Put a quarter of a pound of butter at the bottom of a large cauldron, then lay in the meat and bones, with four ounces of anchovies, and two ounces of mace. . ..'' After adding vegetables, cooking for some hours, straining, reducing, drying in flat dishes (easier, apparently, in frosty weather), we are left with what? Stock cubes!

A standard serving of soup is 7 fluid ounces, and so 1½ imperial pints (= 30 fluid ounces) allows four helpings, with a few spoonfuls over in the bottom of the saucepan.

Apple Soup

1 oz butter, 1 onion, 1 pint chicken stock, 1 level dessertspoon curry powder, 1 level tablespoon cornflour, ¼ pint cream, 2 egg yolks, 2 eating apples, juice of half a lemon, cider or calvados, and parsley.

Chop the onion and fry in butter until golden yellow; stir in the curry powder and the stock. Grate or chop the apples and blend in the cornflour, liquidize, add to the stock and onions and bring to the boil. Stirring frequently, simmer for 15 minutes. Allow to cool a little before adding the cream and egg yolks, well mixed. Stir over a gentle heat until the soup is slightly thickened. Do not allow it to boil. Check the seasoning and add a wine-glass of cider or a spoonful of calvados before serving.

Iced Avocado Soup

James Hay, a Covent Garden porter, showed a friendly interest in seeking out recipes. In a box of avocados that had come from Israel he found this recipe.

1 ripe avocado, 1 small carton sour or fresh cream, 1 tablespoon dry sherry, ¼ pint milk, ½ pint chicken stock, juice from ½ lemon, and some parsley.

Scoop out the flesh of the avocado and mash it with some lemon juice, cream, salt, pepper and sherry. Stir in milk and stock until you have a good, creamy consistency. Cover, chill and serve with a sprinkling of chopped parsley.

Covent Garden Soup

Mr. Gonzales of the Neal Street Restaurant made me a delightful soup, buying about ten different fresh vegetables then in season. He chopped them very finely, braised them lightly in butter and finished cooking them by simmering in plain water, lightly seasoned. The result was a fresh-tasting summer soup.

Iced Cucumber Soup

This soup involves no cooking. Grate a cucumber and mix it with a pint of yogurt, or some milk, a crushed clove of garlic, a teaspoon of tarragon, a tablespoon of wine or cider vinegar, salt and pepper. Sprinkle with chopped mint before serving.

Kenn Soup *(made with Jerusalem Artichokes)*

Clean and then stew four Jerusalem artichokes and an onion in a pint of stock or water until tender. Mix two egg yolks into a cupful of milk. Take the soup off the heat, liquidize or sieve the vegetables, stir in the milk mixture and reheat, stirring until it thickens, but do not let it boil again.

Borsch

Grate a pound of raw beetroot and sweat it in a pan with some butter (1½ oz), add a pint of water or stock and cook until the beetroot is tender (the length of time depends on the age of the beetroot). At this stage the soup can be blended with a liquidizer or passed through a sieve. Add a minced or grated onion, reheat the soup, adjust the seasoning and, just before serving, stir in ¼ pint of sour cream. In the middle of Europe, the home of borsch, the beetroot is slightly fermented in the same way as sauerkraut; the soup then tastes that much more sour.

Belgian Red Cabbage Soup

¼ lb finely chopped red cabbage, 1 oz butter, 1½ pints meat stock, ½ teaspoon sugar, 1 clove garlic, 1 bay leaf, 1 small tart apple chopped finely and 1 potato chopped finely.

Melt the butter in the soup saucepan, sauté the onion, add the cabbage, stir, cover and cook over a low heat for 10 minutes. Add the stock, the crushed garlic, bay leaf, salt, pepper and sugar. Bring to the boil and simmer covered for half an hour. Add the apple and potato and cook for another half hour.

White Cabbage Soup

Cut the cabbage into strips and add it to 1½ pints of boiling water or stock with 1 oz butter, a little chopped onion, carrot, celery and any available green vegetable, such as leek, peas or sliced lettuce. Boil covered for 1½ hours. Season with salt and pepper and a little brown sugar. Cover the bottom of a soup tureen with stale bread leaving the crust on; pour the soup over it, cover it for a few minutes, while the bread gets well soaked, and then serve.

Carrot Soup

Scrape and cut up 1 lb carrots, then put them into a saucepan with a little chopped onion, and celery and 1 oz of butter. Simmer these ingredients in half a pint of milk until they are soft enough to mash together. Add a pint of stock and heat gently until the soup just boils.

Cream of Cauliflower Soup

1 small cauliflower, 1¼ pints bouillon, ½ glass milk, 3 oz butter, and 3 egg yolks.

Only the white parts of the cauliflower are used; simmer these in the bouillon until soft, when the soup can be blended in the liquidizer or pushed through a sieve. Without reheating, stir in the milk and butter and check the seasoning. To thicken, beat the egg yolks with a little water and stir into the soup, heating gently until creamy. Do not allow to boil.

A friend who hates cauliflower was given this soup by his wife who found it in Elizabeth David's *French Provincial Cooking.* He loved it.

Celeriac Soup

Prepare and chop ½ lb celeriac and stew it in a pint of water for 20 minutes. Add ½ lb of sliced potatoes and continue cooking for the same time again. Liquidize, sieve or mash the vegetables in the broth and before serving stir in a good lump of butter or cream or milk.

Celery Soup

Chop a small head of celery and a small onion, and put into a saucepan with an ounce of butter; gently braise for about 10 minutes, then simmer with a pint of stock and seasoning for a further hour. The soup may be thickened by mixing cornflour with a little water and then, while stirring briskly, slowly adding sufficient of this mixture to give the desired consistency. Add a cupful of milk but do not allow the soup to come to the boil again. A blob of cream and some chopped almonds give a touch of glamour.

Chestnut Cream Soup

6 oz chestnuts, 1 pint stock, 1 oz butter, ½ oz flour, 4 glasses of sherry and a little cream.

Slit the chestnuts and boil them in water for 10 minutes and then shell and peel them one by one, leaving the others in the hot water (this is a bit painful until you get used to it). Put the nuts into a saucepan with the stock. Cover and bring to the boil, simmer for 1 hour, take off the heat and then liquidize the nuts or push them through a sieve and return to the stock. To thicken, mix the flour in a little water in a cup to make a thin cream and add this in stages to the soup off the boil. Bring back to the boil, stirring continuously, and repeat if necessary to adjust the degree of thickness. Season to taste and continue cooking for a few minutes. Before serving add the sherry and the cream.

Chestnut Soup *(A manuscript from Sussex dated 1809)*

"Boil a few chestnuts till they bust open. Peel them, crush them into a paste (moistening with a little milk when desireable). Put them through a fine sieve. Set them in a pan with an onion already cooking in a little butter. Add a teaspoonful of sugar, a saltspoonful of salt, a little pepper, a light hint of spice and as much milk as will make up the required amount. Stir continuously, and when it boils, add a spoonful of rice flour, made smooth in cold milk, and a little cream if possible."

Fennel Soup

Simmer a good piece of fennel (half a large one), chopped fine, in 1½ pints of chicken stock until tender (1 hour). To thicken, beat 2 egg yolks with a few drops of lemon juice and blend in some of the hot broth. Add this to the broth in the saucepan off the boil. Reheat, stirring continuously, but do not let it boil.

Garlic Soup

Over a gentle heat render down 6 cloves of garlic, peeled and chopped, together with ½ oz of butter or a dessertspoonful of oil. Add salt, pepper, ½ bay leaf, 1 clove, a sprig of parsley, ¼ teaspoon of thyme and sage mixed and a flick of nutmeg. Pour a pint of hot water over the mixture and simmer for half an hour. As if making mayonnaise, beat a tablespoonful of oil drop by drop into one egg yolk. Strain the hot liquor and whisk a ladleful into the egg and oil, then pour back into the saucepan but do not let it boil again. The soup should be served onto a slice of bread crisped or toasted that has been spread with the egg white, and is improved by a sprinkling of Parmesan cheese.

Leek and Potato Soup

Finely slice the white parts of 2 leeks, 1 small onion and brown them lightly in 1 oz of butter and then add 2 medium potatoes, peeled and also finely sliced. Wash the coarse green parts of the leeks and cook them in 1 pint of chicken stock. Add the stock liquid to the onion and leeks and boil gently for half an hour. Sieve or liquidize and check the seasoning.

This is a very useful soup base: add watercress and you have watercress soup, or allow it to cool and stir in ¼ pint of cream and chill it for Vichyssoise.

Mushroom Soup

1 pint stock, ¼ lb mushrooms, 1 egg, 2 oz cream, 2 mint leaves, ½ oz butter, lemon juice, ¼ teaspoon thyme.

Beat the egg into the cream. Slice the mushrooms and cook them gently with the butter, the chopped mint, thyme, the juice of half a lemon, and a tablespoonful of the stock for 4 minutes. Add some salt and pepper, then mix the mushroom mixture into the cream and egg and slowly add to this the heated stock. Reheat the completed soup, stirring until it blends and thickens but do not let it boil.

Okra Soup

½ lb of okra are cut into one-inch pieces and simmered with a half clove of garlic for about 20 minutes, in 1½ pints of white or chicken stock. Add 2 peeled and chopped tomatoes and cook for another 10 minutes. Adjust the seasoning and serve. This can be served cold.

White Onion Soup

½ lb onions, ½ lb potatoes, ¾ pint stock, ½ pint milk, 2 oz butter.

Chop the onions very small and cook them gently in the butter without letting them brown. Peel the potatoes, cut them into small pieces and add them to the onions and butter. Add the stock, stir well, cook the mixture gently until the potatoes disintegrate and thicken the soup. Thin it down with milk; reheat and season with salt and pepper.

Brown Onion Soup

Cook 1 lb of sliced onions in some butter and oil, about 1½ oz: in all, with a pinch of sugar and some salt and pepper. A full flavour to match the deep rich appearance of this soup is achieved by cooking them slowly, covered, so that they take about half an hour. To turn golden brown, 1 oz of flour is then stirred in and cooked for three minutes. Take the saucepan off the heat and blend in one pint of brown stock, simmer for another half hour then add a tablespoonful of white wine and 2 oz of grated Parmesan cheese. The soup is served by floating a piece of toast spread with crushed garlic and about ½ oz of Parmesan cheese in each soup plate, browned for a minute or two under a hot grill.

Green Pea Soup *(From an 18th-century Essex manuscript)*

"Half a pint of shelled peas, one quart of the green shells, one and a half pints of water, two ounces of butter, one onion, two sprigs of mint, two lumps of sugar, half a pint of milk, one teaspoonful of cornflour. Shell the peas, rinse the empty shells, and with a sharp knife remove the strings. Melt the butter in a clean saucepan, put in the peas, the prepared shells, the onion sliced, and toss (to absorb the flavour of the butter) over a slow fire for a few minutes *but do not brown.* Then add the water, mint, sugar and boil until tender. Rub all through a hair sieve. Blend the cornflour smoothly with the milk. Put the soup back into the saucepan, add the milk and cornflour and stir until it boils. Season and serve, fried croutons of bread should be handed with this soup."

Cream Green Pea Soup

Melt 2 oz butter in a soup saucepan and put in half a lettuce sliced finely. Add 1 lb of shelled peas, salt and a sprinkling of sugar. Stir, cover the pan and leave to cook slowly for 10 minutes. Add 1 pint of water and cook the peas until quite tender. Liquidize or sieve and the soup is ready. Serve with a few chopped chives on top.

Peanut Soup

10 oz roasted peanuts, ½ pint milk, ½ pint light stock, 1 oz butter, 1 oz flour and 1 oz onion.

Chop the onion and grind the peanuts to a fine paste. Simmer 4 dessertspoons of this paste with the milk and the onion for 1 hour. In another saucepan, melt the butter and stir in the flour. Gradually add the stock and finally the peanut mixture. Simmer for 10 minutes. Strain it if you wish. Add a drop of sherry and serve.

Potato Soup

Boil 1 lb of chopped potatoes with a chopped onion and some celery in a pint of water. When tender (30 minutes), liquidize or pass through a sieve and then cook further with some butter, pepper and salt. Before serving remove from the heat and stir in a tablespoonful of cream or some milk. Try sprinkling with chopped chives or parsley.
    Mrs Eve Patrick, a resident of Drury Lane, makes potato soup for the Covent Garden

Community Association. She finishes by stirring in a heaped teaspoonful of tumeric. "This gives it a kick, clears the head and warms the cockles of the heart."

There are two beautifully concise recipes, the first from Ireland:

"Two onions, three potatoes, two ounces of bacon, all sliced thin, pepper and salt. Two pints of water. Boil two hours."

The second recipe is an 18th-century one from Essex:

"Two sticks of celery, one carrot, one onion, one parsely root and some leek. Boil together in some stock with a little butter. Take some floury potatoes, cook, and rub through a hair sieve. Boil with the other ingredients."

Pumpkin Soup

Peel and seed a 1 lb slice of pumpkin, cut the flesh into small pieces and put them into the soup saucepan. Add a finely-chopped stick of celery, ½ pint of milk, 1 pint of light or fish stock, salt and pepper and bring gently to the boil and simmer until the pumpkin is tender (30 minutes). Liquidize or sieve the mixture; add a little lemon juice and a knob of butter before serving. This soup is very good with prawns or small pieces of fish cooked in it for the last 10 minutes.

Spinach Soup

Wash 1 lb of spinach and cook it with ½ a cup of stock. Mash or liquidize the spinach and add ½ pint of cream and milk mixed, a crushed clove of garlic, salt, pepper and two tablespoons of white wine or sherry. To serve hot, do not allow the soup to boil again, but this soup is usually preferred when it is served cold.

Tarragon Soup

Heat 1½ pints of good chicken or light meat stock, add 3 teaspoons of finely chopped fresh tarragon, salt and pepper to taste, then simmer for 10 minutes. Before serving you can stir in some cream. If you like a thicker soup boil chopped potatoes in the stock and mash or liquidize them.

Tomato Soup

In every kitchen in Italy, a hand-operated machine can be found which is wonderfully effective in separating skin and seeds of tomatoes from the flesh and which makes an instant tomato purée which is quite fresh. In the absence of this machine, if the seeds are considered objectionable, some trouble can be taken to peel and sieve the tomatoes. It is possible with ripe tomatoes, if they are cut in half across the direction of the stem, to squeeze the seeds out. Tomatoes are best peeled either by blanching for thirty seconds in boiling water or by rotating on the end of a fork in a gas flame.

A very fresh tomato soup can be made by rendering, down over a gentle heat 1 lb of peeled and sliced tomatoes to which a clove of garlic and some fresh parsley or basil has been added. After a few minutes, mix in 2/3 of a pint of stock, some sugar, salt, pepper, and then simmer for a few more minutes. A small pinch of ground cloves may be an acceptable flavouring for tomato soup.

Tomato soup is very good when served onto sliced hard-boiled egg. It is often served with croutons, which may simply be squares of fried bread.

Italian Tomato Soup

1 lb of tomatoes, skinned, seeded and chopped are fried with some finely chopped onion, celery and parsley, and some garlic, salt and pepper. After 10 minutes add cubes of bread or mix in some flour to thicken the soup. Add about an equal volume of hot water or stock and simmer for one hour, stirring to prevent sticking.

Tomato Soup with Mint *(from Mr Gonzales of Neal Street)*

Choose ripe tomatoes, peel them and strain the seeds out of them. Mix them to your taste with salt, pepper, garlic and chopped mint. Chill for 2-3 hours and serve it plain; just like that.

Cucumber soup can be made in a similar way.

Belgian Turnip Soup

Prepare and dice ¾ lb turnips and cook slowly with a chopped onion, a sprinkling of brown sugar, salt and pepper. After 10 minutes mix in a dessertspoonful of flour and cook for a few more minutes before adding one pint of stock. Simmer for 30 minutes, stirring often. Remove from heat, add cream or milk and serve with fried croutons.

Soup Bonne Femme *(A cream vegetable soup)*

½ lb potatoes, 1 large carrot, 1 large leek, 1 oz butter, 1 pint water, dessertspoonful of cream or the top of the milk, some parsley or chervil and ½ teaspoon sugar.

Melt the butter and add the carrot and leek cleaned and chopped finely. Cook for 5 minutes then add the potatoes, peeled and chopped finely, the water, sugar and seasoning to taste. Bring to the boil and simmer for half an hour. Liquidize or sieve the mixture and when you are ready to serve it add the cream and the chervil or parsley, chopped very finely. This soup is also good cold.

Gazpacho

1 clove garlic, 1 green pepper, 1 onion, 4 ripe tomatoes, ¼ cucumber, 3 tablespoons olive oil, 1 tablespoon vinegar, 1 tablespoon red wine and 1 pint iced water.

Chop all the vegetables (skin the tomatoes before chopping them), saving a little of each for garnishing. Liquidize all the vegetables with the oil, vinegar and wine. Add the water and season well. Leave to chill. Put the chopped pieces into separate bowls and pour the soup over them to serve.

Genovese Vegetable Soup

Chop some cabbage, lettuce, Brussels sprouts, red cabbage, parsley and beetroot. Cover with water and cook until tender with a little salt. Add an equal quantity of milk, and simmer for a few minutes. To this soup add *pesto*, which is basil, two cloves of garlic and grated cheese mixed in a mortar or liquidized together with enough oil to make a thick but runny paste. Put half the paste in with the soup to cook for another ten minutes and save the other half to add just before serving.

Strasbourg Soup *(with lettuce and cucumber)*

A small lettuce chopped together with chopped parsley, cucumber, onion, some chervil, tarragon, salt, pepper, a ½ teaspoon of sugar and a sprinkling of nutmeg are braised for a quarter of an hour together with an ounce of butter. Mix in a dessertspoonful of flour and cook for three minutes before adding a pint of stock. Stir until boiling, then simmer gently for up to half an hour. Before serving, some cream can be stirred in. The delicate flavour of this soup makes it delicious when eaten cold.

Lettuce Soup

A simpler lettuce soup, which is excellent in summer when lettuces are plentiful, is made by simmering a chopped lettuce with chicken stock until tender and then liquidizing and seasoning the soup to taste. Before serving, flavour with nutmeg and add milk, a little butter and some cream if available.

Vegetable Soup

1 onion, 1 leek, 2 sticks of celery, 1 potato, 2 carrots, 3 oz butter or oil, 1 pint stock and 4 tomatoes.

Peel the tomatoes, prepare all the vegetable and cut them up carefully if you want it to look pretty or in ugly lumps if you like to liquidize it. Heat the butter and gently fry all the vegetables. Pour on the stock, bring to the boil, and simmer for about one hour.

The beginnings of the market, 1786

The life of INIGO JONES

HONORIS FANUM

Born in 157_ of a poor cloth-worker, Inigo Jones rose to be architect-general to "4 mighty Kings, 2 heroick queens, & that illustrious & never-to-be-forgotten Prince Henry." His portrait was painted by his good friend, Anthony Van Dyck.

After extensive travels in Italy studying art and architecture at his lordly patron's expense, Jones returned to England with the reputation of a master of rare stage designs & devices and was employed in 1604 designing the Royal Masques

Ben Jonson, who had the temerity to think his plays of equal importance to Jones's devices, bitterly satirised him in one Masque. But Jones had sufficient influence at Court to have the part suppressed at a cost of £2.0s.0d.

Mackie

Appointed Surveyor of Works by King James in 1615; Jones's best-known achievements were the Banqueting House at Whitehall, the rebuilding of the West Portico of St. Paul's, the fashionable Piazza in Covent Garden, & St. Paul's, Covent Garden, "the handsomest barn in England, which was built in the 1630s.

of his theory that Stonehenge was a Roman temple to the god Caelus, the kindest thing said was that his skill as a courtier had led him to provide "ingenious illustrations of the hypothesis of his learned Sovereign, James I, who had commissioned the Stonehenge study".

The Civil War deprived Jones of his patrons & work. He was captured fighting for the King, imprisoned and fined. He did not survive the Commonwealth, but died in 1652, aged 79, having assured his last years and left £100 for a monument of white marble by burying his money secretly by night in Lambeth Marshes

VEGETABLES

ARTICHOKE

"Artichokes agree in COLD WEATHER with old People, and such as are of a phlegmatic and melancholy Temper."

Treatise of all sorts of Foods etc.
M.L. Lemery
London, 1745

Known also as a globe artichoke or French artichoke, this thistle has been cultivated as a delicacy from ages past in the Mediterranean area. In Europe, it is a summer and autumn vegetable and can be eaten whole when young, or in parts when more mature. When very young, it is sometimes eaten uncooked. Usually an hors d'oeuvre, it has a very definite, stony taste and it is rather difficult to think of a drink that would go well with it, particularly a wine.

Artichokes Boiled

Wash the artichokes and put them into boiling water containing a little salt and some lemon juice. Avoid aluminium pans as this may turn them a grey colour. They will cook in about half an hour. You can tell when they are ready because the leaves pull out easily. Serve hot with melted butter or with Hollandaise sauce or Maltaise sauce (a Hollandaise sauce to which is added some juice from an orange, preferably a blood orange, and some grated peel). Artichokes are also good with lemon added to a Hollandaise sauce.

Artichokes Fried

When they are young and tender the leaves will not be at all spiny and it does not matter which sort they are — the tiny ones or the medium violet-tinted ones. To prepare, use scissors to cut off the top, the stem and all the tips of larger outer leaves. Put the artichokes into a deep pan and pour in olive oil until it comes halfway up then cover with lemon juice and water. Allow the mixture to boil quite rapidly — the water and the oil will amalgamate; leave it boiling and spluttering for about 20 minutes by which time the artichokes should be cooked and look like crisp golden flowers. Sprinkle with salt and eat hot.

Braised Artichokes

When cooking artichokes in this Italian manner, use small artichokes trimmed of stem tops and outer leaves. Put the number you need into a pan that they nearly fill, cover with a mixture of equal parts olive oil, white wine or cider and stock; stew gently for an hour covered. Remove the lid and let the liquid boil away at the end, just leaving a little oil.

Artichoke Fritters

Cut off the stems and all the hard leaves and then cut each artichoke lengthways in 8 or 10 pieces. Take out the pieces of choke, the hairy pieces above the heart. Boil in salted lemon water for about 15 minutes. Drain, dry and dip in frying batter and fry in deep hot fat. Sprinkle with salt and eat hot.

Artichoke Hearts

A great delicacy. Choose the largest artichokes available. It is troublesome but not too difficult to cut out the hearts. Boil the hearts very gently in lemon and water until just tender.

Melt butter in a frying pan and cook until soft two shallots or one small onion. Add the artichoke hearts cut into quarters and cook very slowly until all the butter is absorbed. Season to taste.

Buttered artichokes are delicious with poached eggs or omelettes, or they make other vegetables such as carrots or celery into a grander meal. In a Mornay sauce (cheese), to which ham and mushrooms can be added, they make a splendid main course.

Artichokes Stuffed

You will need young and tender artichokes. Cut away the stem, outer leaves and the top. Then scoop out the choke, the hairy piece above the heart. All the stuffings used with aubergines are good for artichokes and the cooking is the same.

ASPARAGUS

"Asparagus is a delicate fruite, and wholesome for everiebodie, and especially when it is thicke, tender and sweete, and no verie much boiled, it giveth good stomach unto the sicke . . . . . , it maketh a good colour in the face."

Maison Rustique 1600.

"Having scraped all the stalks very carefully till they look white, cut all the stalks even alike, throw them into water, and have ready a stewpan boiling. Put in some salt, and tie the asparagus in little bunches. Let the water keep boiling, and when they be a little tender take them up. If you boil them too much, they will lose both their colour and taste. Cut the round off a small loaf about half an inch thick, and toast it brown on both sides. Then dip it into the liquor the asparagus was boiled in, and lay it on your dish. Pour a little butter over your toast, then lay your asparagus on the toast all round your dish, with the white tops outwards. Send up your butter in a bason and do not pour it over your asparagus, as that will make them greasy to the fingers."

From "The London Art of Cookery and Housekeepers complete Assistant", 1783

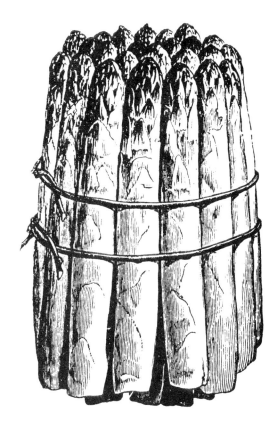

The thick white asparagus needs the outer dry skin of the stalks peeling off with a sharp knife, but the delicious skinny green sticks need no preparation before cooking. Rather than "throwing" your bundles in, stand them carefully upright with the delicate tips upper most and clear of the water. It rarely takes more than 20 minutes to cook.

Asparagus, cooked freshly, is too good not to eat on its own, usually as a starter. When hot, the sauce to choose, is the rich egg yolk and buttery Hollandaise sauce or its variations:

Sauce Mousseline — Hollandaise with whipped cream folded in before serving.

Sauce Maltaise — Hollandaise with added orange juice and grated peel, or Hollandaise with lemon juice and grated peel.

Served cold, various salad dressings are usual:

Vinaigrette — try lemon juice instead of vinegar.

Mayonnaise

Old English Salad Dressing or herb vinaigrette — made with a good vinaigrette in which available fresh herbs have been marinated for two days.

Asparagus with Parmesan Cheese

Wash the asparagus and cut off any hard ends. Boil for 15 minutes in salted water. Drain and cut into inch pieces, sprinkle with parmesan cheese, dot with butter and season to taste. Continue building up layers until all the asparagus has been used. Brown in a moderate oven.

Asparagus Mould

Blanched asparagus, with onion and cheese, cooked with milk and eggs will set in a mould and turned out onto a plate can be served either cold, or hot with a Hollandaise sauce.

2 lbs of asparagus are boiled for 15 minutes in salted water. An onion is finely chopped and slowly cooked in a little butter. Mix together the onions, 2 oz grated cheese, 2 oz breadcrumbs, 3 eggs, ¼ pint of hot milk with 1 oz of butter added, a pinch of nutmeg, salt and pepper. After beating this mixture, add the asparagus and turn into a mould or bowl that has been coated with oil and breadcrumbs. Stand the mould in a tray of water and cook in a preheated slow oven for 30 — 40 minutes. A knife stuck in will come out clean if the cooking is complete.

After standing for 5 minutes, cover the mould with a plate and turn the whole upside down.

Asparagus Tart

Make a mixture with the same ingredients as are used for the asparagus mould but with no breadcrumbs. Put into an open pastry case and bake in a moderately hot preheated oven until a knife stuck in comes out dry, and the top is golden (25 minutes). The taste improves as it cools.

The Piazza, 1630

AUBERGINE

Called egg-plants in English, perhaps because of their shape (and some varieties are white instead of deep purple), they also have the appearance and something of the taste of a rather overcooked omelette when fried. They are a typically Mediterranean food, a characteristic taste in ratatouille and moussaka.

Aubergines Sauté

Cut 3 or 4 medium-sized unpeeled aubergines into ½ inch slices, salt them, leave to drain for at least one hour and then dry them well. Heat some olive oil, add the aubergine slices and let them fry gently until the aubergines are lightly browned. Season with pepper and chopped garlic. Turn a few more times until the cooking is finished; this should take about 15 minutes in all and use up all the oil. If any is left at the end, drain it off.

Aubergines Stewed with Tomatoes

Sauté the aubergines and when cooked and all the oil is used up add about 1 lb of skinned and chopped tomatoes and a teaspoon of fresh or dried basil. Continue cooking until the tomatoes are reduced to a pulpy, not too liquid sauce.

Aubergines Sautéed with Onion

Cut the aubergines into ¼ inch slices, drain and dry. Fry them in hot olive oil until they are just golden brown on both sides, then remove them from the pan. In the same pan, fry the same number of large or medium onions: if the aubergines were large, use large onions. When the onions are soft and a light golden colour, take them out of the pan. Return the aubergines to the pan and spread the onions on top. Season each layer with salt and pepper and a pinch of allspice. Cover and cook over a gentle heat for 15 minutes, or in a pre-heated, moderate oven for about 40 minutes.

Aubergine Purée

I have had this dish with the name "Sugar Daddy" and it does taste very much like a treat, a little bit nutty, almost like nougat but absolutely delicious with flat Greek bread.

Grill or bake 4 aubergines until they are soft and then peel them. Sieve or liquidize the flesh and mix it with 2 tablespoons of yogurt, the same amount of olive oil, some crushed garlic, lemon juice, salt and pepper.

Stuffed Aubergines

Stuffed aubergines make an excellent hors d'oeuvre, or a main dish. They are equally good hot or cold.

Cut 4 largish aubergines in half lengthways, make some cuts in the flesh, but none within ¼ inch of the skin. Sprinkle with salt, press and drain for 1 hour, at least. Dry well and then cut and scoop out the inner flesh, leaving a canoe of skin, ¼ inch thick. Chop up the cut-out flesh and save this to mix with the stuffing.

When the stuffing is ready, pack it gently but firmly back into the aubergine shell. Pour oil over and cook in a slow oven for about an hour.

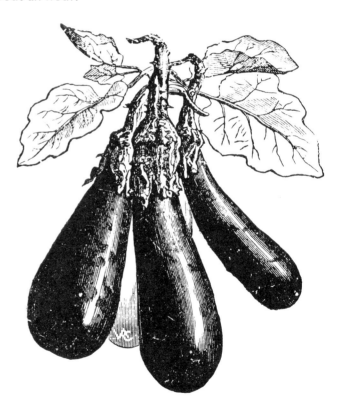

Stuffings:

Anchovy
For this Italian recipe you need 4 oz of bread without a crust, 8 anchovy fillets chopped fine, a dozen black olives, a tablespoon of marjoram or oregano, 2 tablespoons of parsley, 2 or 3 cloves of crushed garlic and same capers. Moisten the bread with wine, water or milk and then mix this with all the other ingredients and the chopped aubergine flesh. Season the mixture with ground black pepper.

Cheese, Ham and Mushroom in Cream Sauce
Prepare ½ pint Béchamel sauce. Make the sauce good and thick. Add the flesh of 6 chopped up aubergines, 4 oz chopped mushrooms, 4 oz chopped ham, 1½ oz grated cheese, a couple of tablespoons of sherry, wine or cider and season to taste, adding some thyme. Fill the aubergines and sprinkle more cheese on top.

Meat
¼ lb sausage meat or uncooked minced meat, 1 oz butter, 1 small onion chopped finely, 2 tablespoons chopped parsley. Melt the butter and add to it the onion and when this is soft, the rest of the ingredients, including the aubergine flesh. Cook until the meat is browned and the whole mixture hot, then stuff the shells.

Baked Aubergines

Take whole unpeeled aubergines, cut them like slicing a loaf of bread, but only halfway down. Make each slice about ¼ inch thick. Into these slices, poke alternately small pieces of bacon and chopped garlic, mixed with salt and pepper and basil or marjoram. If you carefully poke the stuffing down with a knife, it sinks well into the vegetable. Put the aubergines in a baking dish and pour oil over them. Put into a pre-heated slow oven for about an hour.

Aubergine Fritters

Cut the aubergines into rounds if they are large, or long slices of they are smaller. Do not cut the slices any thicker than ¼ inch·or they will not cook. Salt and drain. The batter also improves with time so it is a good idea to make it first.
 Dip the slices in the batter and cook in oil until they are crisp and golden. This only takes 3 or 4 minutes. Sprinkle with salt. They can be served with lemon.

Melanzani alla Parmigiana

Giovanni's is an Italian restaurant in Goodwin's Court, near the site of the Pineapple Tavern frequented by Dr. Johnson:

> "I dined very well for eight pence with very good company, at the Pineapple in New Street. Several of them had travelled — they expected to meet every day, but did not know one anothers names. It used to cost the others a shilling, for they drank wine; but I had a cut of meat for 6d, and bread for a penny and gave the waiter a penny; so that I was quite well served, aye! better than the rest, for they gave the waiter nothing."

Giovanni himself comes from Parma, the home of Parmesan cheese, the best of the hard, matured cheeses for grating and for seasoning food. He was pleased to give us a recipe from his own province:

Three good-sized egg plants are sliced lengthways into ¼ inch slices and fried in oil until golden brown and then seasoned with salt and pepper. Put a layer in a dish and cover with thin slices of Mozzarella cheese, some tomato sauce and a sprinkling of Parmesan cheese. Fill the dish with layer upon layer and end up with a more liberal sprinkling of Parmesan cheese. Cook in a moderate oven until hot all through (20 minutes) and then brown the top lightly under the grill.

Moussaka

3 medium aubergines	1 crushed garlic clove
¾ lb onions	salt and pepper
½ pint olive oil (approx.)	7 fl. oz stock (just under ½ pint)
1-1¼ lb minced raw lamb or mutton, beef will do.	½ teaspoon sugar
	1 dessertspoon tomato paste
pinch of cinnamon	½ pint Béchamel sauce
3 tablespoons chopped parsley	4 tablespoons grated cheese

Cut aubergines into slices, about ¼ inch thick, salt and put aside to drain. Dry them and then fry gently in olive oil. When they are soft, remove from the oil. Put in the onions, finely chopped, adding more oil if needed. When the onions begin to colour, add the meat, cinnamon, parsley, sugar and garlic. Cook until the meat is brown.

Cover the bottom of an ovenproof dish with a layer of aubergines, follow with a layer of cooked mixture — continue the layers, seasoning with salt and pepper, as you go. Finish with a layer of aubergines. Warm the stock and add it to the tomato paste. Pour this over the layers and cook in a slow oven for about one hour.

Make the Béchamel sauce and add 3 tablespoons of cheese. Cover the aubergine layer with the sauce and sprinkle the last spoonful of cheese over it. Turn the oven up to moderate and cook until the top is brown (20 minutes).

Aubergine Pizza

Thinly slice one unpeeled medium aubergine and place the slices in a very lightly oiled shallow baking dish. Make the sauce to cover it by mixing together 4 or 5 peeled and chopped tomatoes (if fresh ones are out of season or too expensive canned tomatoes are fine but never use tomato purée), two cloves of crushed garlic, salt and pepper, and a dessertspoonful of olive oil. Spread the mixture over the aubergine and liberally sprinkle with oregano or marjoram, then add to taste some black olives, some capers, and thin slices of Gruyère, Bel Paese or Mozzarella cheese. Bake in a pre-heated moderate oven (20–30 minutes) and finish off under a grill.

The English love pies. Sometimes the crust may go underneath instead of on top. In particular there is bacon and egg pie. As you go south from England the French version is called quiche (for example Quiche Lorraine, an egg and bacon tart). Further south the French quiche becomes the Italian pizza, the egg disappears as an ingredient, and the bacon is replaced by a sharp savoury such as anchovy or salami. In the Italian pizza the pastry is breadlike. The Aubergine pizza sheds the breadcrust and replaces it with slices of aubergine, and so it is not a pizza at all, but it makes a nice name. Neapolitan pizzas are made with a bread dough raised with yeast. The sauce described for the aubergine pizza is right for the Neapolitan pizza, with the addition of anchovies.

AVOCADO

Ahuacatl is a Mexican word for the alligator, and this fruit, which came from South America, was known as the alligator pear. Avocado (= advocate) is a Spanish corruption of the Mexican. Nowadays every tropical country grows some avocado pears but the main exporters to England are Israel, South Africa and East Africa. Generous claims are made for the avocado: the high protein flesh, the vitamins, minerals and cholesterol-free oils and the low sugar content for those who are slimming. But, for all that, it is rather an acquired taste, or rather texture, for in truth it does not at first seem to taste of very much, but definitely provides substance. When there is a choice the smallish, black and warty-looking Hass variety seems always to be the one preferred.

Generally the avocado appears as hors d'oeuvre, cut in half lengthways, the stone removed by a neat trick with a sharp knife where the blade is embedded in the stone and a twist of the blade loosens and removes the stone. The cavities are then filled with dressing. The dressing can be mayonnaise with fish, shellfish or vegetables but good vinaigrette brings out the taste to advantage.

Since avocados are imported rock hard they are often on sale quite unripe. The test for ripeness is the same as for the other sort of pear, pressure from a thumb at the sharp end to see if the flesh yields. Often a boat load of unripe pears does not sell well as there is a glut when they come to readiness as the traders in the market then sell them off quickly. They are then on street traders' barrows throughout London at knockdown prices in a very ripe and ready condition.

Avocado Mousse *(a dip for parties as well)*

2 ripe avocados, ¾ carton sour cream, juice of ½ a lemon,
3 tablespoons sweet sherry or wine

Cut the avocados in half lengthways, remove the stones, and scoop out the flesh with a spoon. Mash the flesh until smooth. Add the cream, lemon and sherry. Mix it all to a smooth, stiff consistency. Keep covered in a fridge or cool place to stop discolouring.

BAMBOO SHOOTS

Bamboo Shoots and French Beans

Break about a pound of beans into 2-inch pieces and cook them in some oil for 2 minutes, stirring frequently. Add a cupful of sliced bamboo shoots, a teaspoonful of salt and sugar and half a cup of water. Cook slowly for ten minutes.

Vegetables cooked in the Chinese manner are crisp to eat and taste better for being slightly undercooked.

"On Friday last Week a Woodcock was taken alive in Covent-Garden Square, and purchas'd by a Gentleman for two Shillings."
Universal Spectator, *7 December 1728*

BROAD BEANS

Broad beans are at their best when really young, the beans no bigger than an old-fashioned sixpence and the furry pods so tender that they too can be eaten easily. Later the pods coarsen and the beans should be removed. It is best to do this after boiling them whole, in their pods.

Put the beans into slightly salted boiling water and cook uncovered, until tender (15 minutes).

Serve with butter or in parsley Béchamel sauce. Add a good handful of chopped parsley to the Béchamel sauce just before it has finished cooking.

They are good cold with mayonnaise, or just olive oil and lemon juice.

Broad beans accompany ham to the advantage of both or chopped ham can be mixed in with a sauce to bring them together. Eggs, say scrambled or as an omelette, seem to be just right with beans.

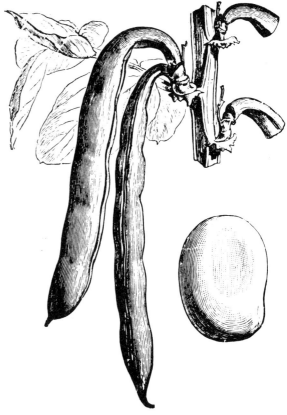

Broad Beans with Green Pepper Sauce

Nito Baez-Falcon is an excellent vegetable cook, perhaps because he comes from the Canary Isles where meat is a rare treat. He cooks in "Food for Thought", a restaurant in Neal Street.

Margot Grainger, who owns the restaurant, has proved you can serve a wide range of good food without having to use, or pretent to use, meat or fish. This is Nito's recipe:

Boil the beans until they are nearly tender. Leave them off the heat, in just enough of the water to cover. Make a sauce by frying onions until they are soft and then adding lots of seeded green peppers, cut small, chopped parsley and garlic, salt and pepper and a bouquet garni. Fry all the ingredients together for 3 or 4 minutes then tip them into the beans and water and boil together for about ½ an hour, or until the liquid has boiled off enough to leave the beans in a dressing. Take out the bouquet garni and serve.

BEAN SPROUTS

Mung beans can sometimes be bought in Chinese or Indian shops. Soak them in cold water for several hours and then wrap them in a damp kitchen towel, keeping them warm and in the dark for a few days. Toss the beans in the towel from time to time to stop them rooting in the towel. The most convenient place to keep them wrapped in their towel is in a colander. One cup of beans makes about a pound of bean sprouts.

The sprouts, removed from the beans and washed, may be dropped into boiling salted water and cooked for about 2 minutes and then served with a little butter or oil and soy sauce.

If you like ginger, cook a pound of bean sprouts in some oil with 2 or 3 chopped spring onions, a ½ teaspoon of ground ginger and a tablespoon of soy sauce. Cook for 3 or 4 minutes, stirring frequently.

FRENCH BEANS

A South American native, the French bean is said to have been introduced to an almost beanless Elizabethen England by the Huguenots. Now there are so many beans, apart from the original broad bean, that confusion is assured. The French bean (called string bean in the USA) is eaten whole and eaten young; when mature the pod is discarded and the seed is called a haricot bean. Needless to say, there are stringless varieties of the string bean; in particular there is a yellow one, eaten very young, called a Wax-pod bean, also known as a *mange-tout* and sometimes as a butter bean, perhaps because it is yellow.

About a pound and a half can easily be eaten by four people: they are better steamed than boiled, and to prepare them for cooking simply top and tail them, and put them with some butter or oil and a pinch of salt.

If you think it better or less trouble to boil them do it quickly and stop the moment they taste right (10 minutes).

Hot or cold with olive oil, a little garlic and black pepper, they are delicious.

LIMA BEANS

This variety of bean is a fairly rare South American visitor to Britain but is ubiquitous in the USA. Shelled from its pod and fresh it takes 20 — 30 minutes to cook, usually with onions and herbs. The dried lima bean should be washed, brought to the boil in water, left to soak for 2 hours or more and then cooked slowly for about an hour and a half. A good casserole is made with layers of bacon covered with sliced tomato sprinkled with chopped onion, parsley, basil, salt and pepper, then covered with about half a pound of the beans. Repeat the layer: bacon, tomato, etc, and the same amount of beans again, and then cover with some more tomato and bacon. Put a lid on the casserole and cook until the beans are tender (¾ hour) in a medium oven. Finish the cooking with a further 10 to 15 minutes with the lid removed from the casserole.

BEETROOT

During the summer small young beetroot are at their best and make marvellous salads or a simply prepared and delicious hot vegetable.

It is advisable to buy uncooked beetroot whenever possible as greengrocers often over-cook them. Also really young beetroot are good uncooked.

According to size and age they can take anything from 20 minutes to two hours to boil tender. Do not be anxious and stab them too soon or some of their juices will bleed away. The sweetness of beetroot is usually set off by a little vinegar or lemon juice.

Beetroots Baked in the Oven

Choose medium to large uncooked beetroots, scrub them clean and cook them in the oven the same way as baked potatoes. They take longer, up to 3 hours in a medium oven.

When cooked they can be served hot, like potatoes, cut open with butter, salt and pepper or they can be sliced and dressed with vinegar in the usual way. Baking beetroots makes sense if the oven is already in use for a casserole or roast.

Hot Beetroot with Butter

Just slice and heat up the cooked beetroot with some butter and sprinkle with parsley before serving.

Hot Beetroot with Onion

Slice and cook an onion in plenty of butter. When soft, add sliced cooked beetroot and continue cooking for a few minutes. Sprinkle with lemon juice or vinegar before serving.

Hot Beetroot a la Crême

Prepare the hot beetroot with onion. Before serving add a tablespoonful of cream.

Beetroot in Orange Sauce

A sauce or glaze is made with the juice of an orange, ½ oz butter, and the grated orange rind which are heated in a saucepan. A teaspoon of cornflour blended with a tablespoonful of water is added and the mixture brought to the boil. Stir continuously. Add 1 lb of diced cooked beetroot, stir and cover. Simmer for several minutes. Season with salt and pepper. This is recommended with gammon steaks, cooked ham or bacon.

Hot Glazed Beetroot

Heat vinegar and water and add a little cornflour mixed with water. Stir continuously until boiling. Add this glaze to the hot cooked beetroot. Serve with butter and parsley.

Beet Leaves

Boil the leaves in salted water, then drain, chop and serve them with butter or white sauce.

BROCCOLI

Broccoli, a lovely vegetable, should be cooked with the same care as asparagus. Divide it into pieces of stems with flowers, and any extra stalks or leaves, cut up small. Put the extra stalks first in boiling salted water and then carefully add the pieces with flowers on them, keeping the flowers upwards. Allow about 8 minutes to cook. Drain carefully.

It can be served as a separate course, or as a vegetable to accompany roast poultry or meats, or with egg dishes.

Serve hot with melted butter or with any of the sauces that are good with asparagus.

Cold broccoli can be served with lemon juice and olive oil or with more complicated sauces of the sort that suit asparagus.

Broccoli with cheese can be cooked in the same way as Brussels sprouts and cheese.

Braised Broccoli *(Chinese)*

Cut 1 lb of broccoli into 1 inch pieces. Heat about 1½ tablespoonsful of oil in a large saucepan or frying pan. Quick fry the broccoli for just half a minute, and sprinkle with salt. Stirring gently, add 1 teaspoonful of soya sauce, a teaspoonful of sugar and enough water to stop the broccoli catching on the bottom of the pan. Simmer for 3 or 4 minutes while the water boils away.

BRUSSELS SPROUTS

Midwinter in wind-swept Bedfordshire and the flat countryside seems to offer little; but there is Greene King Abbots Ales, the memory of the huge airships and, last and most of all, some of the best Brussels sprouts. A vegetable for frosty weather, good with poultry and the Christmas turkey, sausages, liver and baked ham. Choose small tightly packed ones, and since they are best cooked fast, slit the bottoms to ensure even cooking and leave the pan uncovered.

Brussels Sprouts Braised in Butter

Part cook the sprouts by dropping into boiling salted water and then cooking slowly for about 6 minutes.

   Put the sprouts in a buttered ovenproof dish. Season with pepper and dot with butter. Heat on the stove until they are just sizzling and then put them into a pre-heated moderate oven and bake until they are tender and have soaked up all the butter (20 minutes).

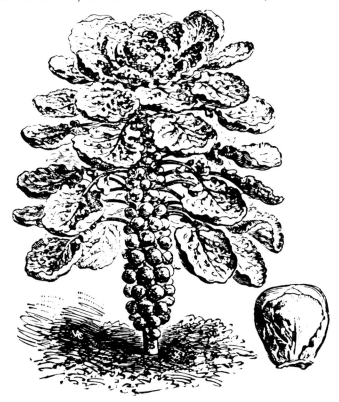

Norman Brussels Sprouts

Braise the sprouts. After they have been in the oven for 10 minutes pour over them ¼ pint of boiling cream and then continue cooking for 10 minutes or until the vegetables are tender. Serve as quickly as possibly.

Brussels Sprouts with Cheese

Braise the sprouts and when they have been in the oven 10 minutes sprinkle on 2 oz of grated cheese (a mixture of Parmesan and Swiss cheese is best) for each pound of sprouts. Shake this through the sprouts and then sprinkle another 2 oz down the sides and over the top. Pour on ½ oz of melted butter. Cook in a hot oven until the cheese is browned and the sprouts tender (another 10 minutes).

Brussels Sprouts Mould

Sprouts can be mixed with milk, cheese, eggs and breadcrumbs, and cooked in a mould, and are very rich if served with a sauce as a separate course. Use the method and ingredients as though making asparagus mould, using lightly cooked then finely chopped sprouts in place of asparagus.

Brussels Sprouts and Chestnuts *(an 18th-century recipe from Devonshire)*

"Boil some chestnuts in water for 2 hours; remove the peel. Boil an equal amount of Brussel Sprouts for half an hour, strain them well; be careful not to break them. Have ready a frying pan with hot dripping or butter, put in both chestnuts and sprouts, and keep them moving until the fat is absorbed (do not brown them); then serve."

(About ½ lb of chestnuts is enough for each pound of sprouts.)

CABBAGE

"Be very careful that your greens be nicely picked and washed, and when so done, always lay them in a clean pan, for fear of sand or dirt, which are apt to hang round wooden vessels. Boil all your greens in well-tinned copper saucepan by themselves, and be sure to let them have plenty of water. Boil no kind of meat with them as that discolour them; and use no iron pans, such being very improper for the purpose, but let them be either copper or brass well tinned, or silver. Numbers of cooks spoil their garden stuffs by boiling tnem too much: all kinds of vegetables should have a little crispness; for if you boil them too much, you will deprive them of both their sweetness and beauty.

"All sorts of cabbage and young sprouts must have plenty of water allowed them to boil in, and when the stalks become tender, or fall to the bottom, it is a proof of their being sufficiently boiled. Then take them off before they lose their colour; but remember always throw some salt into your water before you put in your greens. You must send your young sprouts to table whole as they come out of the pot; but many people think cabbage is best chopped and put into a saucepan with a piece of butter, stirring it about for five to six minutes, till the butter be all melted, then empty it on a dish and serve it up."

> from "The London Art of Cookery and Housekeepers complete Assistant. On a New Plan. Make plain and Easy to the under standing of every housekeeper, cook and servant in the kingdom", John Farley, Dublin, 1783.

Green cabbage and spring greens, when fresh, cook quite quickly, contrary to many expectations. There is not much to add to John Farley's preliminary hints except to wonder whether the lid is best on or off. My answer is to put the lid on crooked, to leave a gap, which achieves rapid cooking by conserving heat while maintaining sufficient ventilation to keep a good colour and fresh taste. Experience shows that cabbage cooks nicely with the minimum amount of water to prevent sticking or burning and this is probably more in line with contemporary thinking about conserving minerals and vitamins. However, for those who drink the cabbage water, it probably works either way.

"Covent Garden, when it was market morning, was wonderful company. The great wagons of cabbages, with growers, men, and boys lying asleep under them and sharp dogs from market garden neighbourhoods looking after the whole, was as good as a party."

Charles Dickens.

"If thou desirest to die, eat cabbages in August."
— The Physician of Myddvai (13th century).

Cabbage Baked with Yogurt

1 carton of yogurt, 1 cabbage (about 1 lb), 4 oz grated cheese (Parmesan or Gruyère is best), and 2 eggs.

Clean and cut a medium sized cabbage into thin slices and boil until it is just cooked but still crisp. Mix one carton of plain yogurt with 2 eggs and 4 oz cheese. Drain the cabbage thoroughly; press it into a colander with a plate, chop it and press it again. Mix the yogurt and eggs into the cabbage in a buttered ovenproof dish and put in at the top of a preheated hot oven until it is baked and the top browned (30 minutes)

This is a useful method for slimmers. It is also a good way of cooking carrots and cauliflower. Butter can be added to make it richer.

White or Dutch Cabbage with Caraway

1 white cabbage about 1 lb in weight, 1 onion, 3 oz lard, dripping or oil, 1 teaspoon caraway seeds and the juice of ½ lemon or a dessertspoon of vinegar.

The trick when cooking red or white cabbage is to get it started without catching it on the bottom of the saucepan, since once warmed up it generates its own cooking juices in sufficient quantity. Melt the fat in the bottom of a thick saucepan and add the grated cabbage and chopped onion with a very little salt and the caraway seeds. Stir until warmed, adding if necessary a moistening of water. Cook for about half to three-quarters of an hour over a low heat stirring occasionally. When tender add the lemon juice or vinegar.

A sprinkling of flour can be stirred in to bind the whole together in a sort of sauce, if desired. Cooking should then be continued until the floury taste has disappeared (10 minutes).

Cabbage cooked like this makes quite a substantial accompaniment to sausages or pork dishes.

Stuffed Cabbage

4 large cabbage leaves, ½ lb sausage meat or 6 oz minced beef with 2 oz cooked rice or breadcrumbs, ½ teaspoon thyme, 1 oz dripping or butter, 1 oz flour and some bouillon or stock.

Choose large leaves in good condition, but not too coarse. Clean them well. Mix the sausage or minced meat with the thyme and add some salt and pepper. Divide the mixture into quarters and roll each up in a cabbage leaf, fold in the sides until the meat is completely parcelled, and then secure with some string. Lay the leaves in one layer in a flameproof dish or in a heavy saucepan and pour the bouillon or stock around them about ½ inch deep. Cover and boil gently for 20 minutes.

Chinese Cabbage

The Chinese cabbage looks more like a white Cos lettuce, and indeed is sometimes called Chinese lettuce. Its real name is Pe-tsai (pe means white and tsai means vegetable). It can be eaten raw like Dutch cabbage. It is very good braised quickly in the Chinese manner or in any way suitable for the common cabbage.

Red Cabbage

Red cabbage is traditionally cooked very slowly for up to 5 hours. It is worth cooking it slowly and properly; it tastes better and the dishes are easy to prepare, needing little or no attention.

It is possible to cheat and boil it fast, drain and then proceed with the recipes, allowing no more time than it takes to mix and heat through the fats, flour or jelly. Red cabbage is always cooked with something acid to retain its colour. It makes a hearty dish to serve with roast goose, duck, pork, partridge or sausages.

The dishes given here are very good cooked beforehand, left covered and reheated the next day.

Red Cabbage with Apples

A small red cabbage is plenty for four people as the vegetable is so dense. After removing the outer leaves and the stalk, chop it finely. Also chop 2 cooking apples or 3 tart eating apples. Put into a heavy saucepan 2 oz butter, 1 tablespoon cider vinegar or some cider with a teaspoon of vinegar, 3 cloves, the cabbage and the apple. Sprinkle the whole with salt and pepper.

Heat the mixture, stirring it once or twice, then lower the heat, cover the pan and leave to simmer for at least 2½ hours.

Before serving, stir in 2 tablespoons of redcurrant jelly and some lemon juice. Serve very hot.

Red Cabbage Baked with Wine and Chestnuts

6 shelled and skinned chestnuts, 1 small carrot finely sliced, 2 oz butter or pork or goose dripping, 1 lb red cabbage cut into ½ inch slices, 1 cooking apple sliced, 1 clove garlic mashed, 1 bay leaf fragmented, ¾ pint red wine (you can use cider), ¾ pint stock or beef bouillon and a thick slice of bacon well chopped.

Heat up the butter or dripping in a casserole and add to it the carrot, onion and bacon; fry these slowly for about 10 minutes without browning them. Stir in the cabbage until it all has a light coating of fat and vegetables, cover and cook slowly for 10 minutes. Stir in all the other ingredients except the chestnuts and bring them to the boil; correct the seasoning, then put the casserole into the centre of a preheated medium oven, regulating the heat so that the casserole bubbles slowly for 3 to 3½ hours. Now add the chestnuts, re-cover and return the casserole to the oven for a final 1 hour's cooking. Frankfurters, added 10 minutes before serving, make this dish into a satisfying meal.

Red Cabbage with Red Wine

1 small red cabbage, ½ cup beef or chicken stock, ½ cup of red wine.

Trim and wipe a small red cabbage and cut into quarters. Boil these for 20 minutes in a closed saucepan with the stock. Add the wine, sprinkle with salt and pepper and cook gently for another 40 minutes. The cabbage will absorb the flavours.

CALABRESE

Also known as asparagus broccoli or green sprouting broccoli, it is a type of broccoli with many little green flower heads. All the recipes for broccoli or cauliflower are suitable for cooking calabrese.

CARDOONS

Cardoons, Cardons, Chardoons, Chard

All names for a thistle artichoke-like plant. The inner stalks and its roots are very pleasant boiled like asparagus and served cold as an hors d'oeuvre or salad, or hot cooked in any way recommended in recipes for celery or asparagus.

Escoffier, the famous chef of the Carlton in London, gives seven recipes for cooking cardoons in his *Guide to Modern Cookery (1907-20).* This is one:

Coeur de Cardon aux Fines Herbes

"Having cooked the heart of the cardoon, trim it all round so as to give it a cylindrical shape, and cut it laterally into roundels one-third inch thick.

"Roll these roundels in some pale, thin, buttered meat glaze combined with chopped herbs. Prepared in this way, the heart of the cardoon constitutes an excellent garnish for tournedos and sautéed chickens."

CARROTS

"A cure for asthma. Live a fortnight on boiled carrots only."

John Wesley, *Primitive Physic*, 1789.

"CARROT JUICE DIET KILLED SCIENTIST

A health food addict who had been drinking up to eight pints of carrot juice a day was bright yellow when he died, an inquest at Croydon, Surrey, was told yesterday. Dr John Fabricius said he believed Mr Basil Brown, aged 48, a scientific adviser, had died of vitamin A poisoning.

Mrs Brenda Brown, of Hayes Lane, Kenley, the dead man's wife, told Dr Mary McHugh, the coroner, that she had prepared the carrot juice. "Nobody prescribed it. He just thought it was the right way to eat. He also took vitamin A tablets."

A typical day's diet for her husband was: breakfast, carrot juice and fruit; midday, more carrot juice and fruit; evening meal, eggs, tomatoes, cheese.

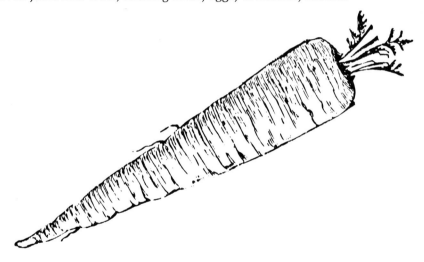

Dr. J. Fabricius, the family's doctor, told the coroner that he had warned Mr Brown against his addiction to vitamin A. He had warned Mr Brown to stop taking vitamin A and had later sent him to a specialist who also warned him. Mr Brown had been "an intelligent man but he had a very low opinion of doctors".

Dr David Haler, a pathologist, said that Mr Brown was bright yellow when he died. Vitamin A poisoning, like alcoholic poisoning, produced cirrhosis of the liver.

The inquest found that Mr Brown had died from carrot juice addiction."

The Times, 15th February 1974

English carrots have a long season, from July onwards through the autumn, winter and spring until May. The first English crop comes tied in bundles; after a month or so they arrive in nets. The gap from May to July is well filled by the Cyprus carrots, very uniform in shape, and with a distinct but pleasant resinous tang.

Finger carrots, looking very appetizing, arrive from Holland during a good part of the colder weather — I never seem to have much luck with them, they seem tasteless and therefore I avoid them.

I find that carrots sliced lengthways cook in much less time than when they are chopped across into discs, but try for yourself.

Carrots Vichy

In a heavy saucepan melt 2 oz of butter and put in 1½ lb of cleaned carrots, cut lengthwise into strips; add one tablespoon of water, salt, a teaspoonful of sugar and some pepper. Allow to simmer very gently for between 30 minutes and an hour, depending on the carrots. Stir occasionally.

Carrots cooked like this are good with meat or they are so good they can be eaten as a separate course. Chopped parsley gives the right extra taste and looks attractive.

It is possible that there is something special about the water of Vichy that makes it particularly good for cooking vegetables. Since it can be bought in bottles you can try for yourself to see whether real Vichy water brings any magic to your cooking.

Hashed Carrots

Clean 1 lb of carrots, then slice and put them into a heavy saucepan with 1 oz of butter, a handful of chopped parsley, salt, pepper and 2 tablespoons of milk. Cook the mixture very gently until tender (50 minutes). Take off the heat, remove the carrots to a serving dish and thicken the remaining liquid with an egg yolk and pour over the carrots before serving.

Braised Carrots and Onions

Equal quantities of onions and carrots braised exactly as the carrots in the Vichy recipe make a delicious and simple vegetable to accompany roasts, grills, stews or pies.

Braised Carrots and Potatoes

Peel the potatoes and cut them into one-inch cubes, scrub the carrots and cut them into the same sized pieces and then cook the two vegetables together exactly as in the Vichy recipe for carrots.

Carrots with Sherry

Vichy carrots prepared with a tablespoonful of sherry added to the tablespoonful of water have a glossy coating of butter and sherry and taste extremely good.

Carrots with Cream Sauce

Cook Vichy carrots, but be mean with the butter and then pour a little boiling cream over them. Shake the pan over the heat for just long enough to allow the cream to thicken.

Carrots with Parsley Sauce

Cook the carrots by the Vichy method or boil them if you are in a hurry. Make ½ pint of Béchamel sauce and add to it a good handful of chopped parsley. Add the carrots to the sauce and keep warm for 2 or 3 minutes before serving.

Carrot Tea Loaf

3 oz butter, 4 oz self-raising flour, 1 teaspoon cinnamon, ¼ lb sugar, ¼ lb grated raw carrots, 2 oz chopped walnuts and 1 egg.

Mix the flour, salt and cinnamon. Cream the butter and sugar together with a fork until they are thick and fluffy, and blend in the egg and beat well. Gradually add and stir in the flour mixture until smooth, finally stirring in the carrots and the nuts. Turn the mixture into a well buttered baking tin and cook in a pre-heated medium oven until the top springs back when pressed lightly with a fork (¾ hour). Turn out and cool on a cake rack.

Carrots à la Concierge

A casserole of carrots, onion and garlic in a cream sauce.

This is quite a substantial dish which could be eaten alone or would go well with plain meat, roast poultry or sausages.

About 1½ lbs of carrots are prepared for cooking (scrubbed and sliced) and put into a covered saucepan together with ½ lb sliced onion and a chopped clove or garlic. Add about an ounce of oil or butter and simmer for half an hour. Stir in a dessertspoonful of flour and cook for a few minutes; add a cupful of hot milk and stock mixed, salt, pepper, a pinch of nutmeg and a teaspoonful of sugar and continue to boil uncovered until the sauce reduces and thickens (20 minutes). Take off the heat and add 2 oz of cream into which 2 egg yolks have been stirred. The sauce will then thicken if stirred over a gentle heat. Turn into a warm dish and sprinkle with parsley.

Carrot Sweetmeat *(Indian)*

1½ pints fresh milk, ¼ lb grated carrots, 5 oz sugar, 2 tablespoons sultanas, 1 teaspoon crushed cardamom seeds or grated nutmeg, 1 teaspoon desiccated coconut, 2 tablespoons finely sliced mixed nuts, 4 oz butter.

Put the milk and carrots into a heavy saucepan or frying pan and boil gently, stirring frequently until the mixture thickens (45 minutes). Add sugar and continue cooking for another 15 minutes. Add the butter and turn the heat right down. If you keep mixing and frying most of the fat will be absorbed; this should take less than 10 minutes. Stir in the sultanas and remove the pan from the heat. Pour off into a shallow buttered dish and decorate with coconut and crushed cardamom seeds or nutmeg. When it is cool cut it into small biscuit-sized pieces.

Baked Carrots

Carrots can be cooked in the same way as roast potatoes in a baking tray with a little fat. They should be left whole. Average size carrots should take about 45 minutes in a hot oven. Take care not to let them overcook because their high sugar content makes them liable to burn.

"My carrots last year were remarkably fine. I sold as much as brought £14 and I am convinced that if I had known Covent Garden as I do now, I should have sold the same weight for near thirty."

Edmund Burke in a letter to Arthur Young, dated 1771.

CAULIFLOWER

This versatile vegetable is a variety of cabbage grown for its flower and is eaten like broccoli, but usually does not have quite as good a flavour. It originated in the Mediterranean, probably Cyprus, but most English cauliflowers come to the market still crated in multiples of the old-fashioned dozen from Norfolk, by the shores of the North Sea. Grated cauliflower is good in salads. Cooked, it can be served on its own with butter or in a variety of sauces. Young cauliflower cooks very quickly and is best steamed. Older tougher ones can be cooked by putting the stalk ends downwards in the saucepan with only enough water for the stalks to sit in, thus boiling the stalks while steaming the flowery parts.

"How to butter a colleflowre. Take a ripe Colleflowre and cut off the buddes, boyle them in milk with a little Mace while they be very tender, then poure them into a Cullender, and let the Milke run cleane from them, then take a ladle full of Creame, being boyled with a little whole Mace, putting to it a Ladle-full of thick Butter, mingle them together with a little Sugar, dish up your Flowres upon Sippets; poure your butter and creame hot upon it, strewing on a little slicst Nutmeg and Salt, and serve it to the Table hot."

John Murrell, *Delightful Daily Exercise for Ladies and Gentlemen,* 1621.

Buttered Cauliflower

Trim the outer leaves, leaving only the inner tender green leaves. Cut the cauliflower into two halves and then into as many wedges as required. Sprinkle with a very little salt and steam for about 15 minutes. Melt some butter and heat until the butter begins to bubble. Add chopped parsley, salt and pepper. Put the cauliflower in the serving dish and pour the butter over it.

Cauliflower Fried in Batter

Lightly steam a cauliflower and divide it into bouquets of two or three flowerets. Season these with pepper, salt, wine or cider vinegar and chopped parsley and chives. They should stand for a few minutes before dipping them in batter and frying in deep fat. They can be served with tomato sauce.

Cauliflower "Alla Piemontese"

Finely chop an onion, a couple of anchovy fillets, a teaspoonful of fresh sweet herbs and cook with some butter, add stock and a little vinegar. Pour this sauce over a freshly steamed cauliflower and keep on the heat for a further few minutes before serving.

Cauliflower Cheese

Pour a Mornay Sauce over freshly steamed wedges of cauliflower. Sprinkle on breadcrumbs, dot with butter and brown in a hot oven or under the grill.

Cauliflower with Garlic and Tomatoes

Finely chop a clove of garlic with a small onion and soften in a saucepan with a tablespoon of oil over a gentle heat. Add ½ lb of skinned and chopped tomatoes, salt, pepper and some basil. Cook a fairly finely sliced small cauliflower in this sauce until tender, adding white wine to make up for the evaporation.

CELERIAC

This turnip-rooted version of celery is available in the Market in winter and its use seems to be on the increase. Usually knobbly and a bit hard to clean, it takes a while to peel. Finely shredded it is good for salads.

Braised Celeriac

Cut into thin strips it braises well in the Chinese manner.

Heat a spoonful of oil in a frying pan and toss the celeriac over a lively heat for about ten minutes. It should be evenly cooked but remain somewhat crisp. Season with salt and pepper and a sprinkle of vinegar.

Celeriac Purée

Boil together equal quantities of potato and celeriac in salted water. When soft, liquidize or mash them through a sieve. Mix in butter, a little milk or cream, salt and pepper to taste. This is an interesting savoury and a good change from plain mashed potatoes with chicken, grilled fish, or cheese dishes.

Fried Celeriac

Peel the celeriac and cut it into tiny chips. Deep fry them until golden brown (4 minutes). Serve hot.

CELERY

This winter vegetable is of European origin and has an important part to play in flavouring stews, ragouts and soups. The season for English grown celery is from the first frosts through until April, but in the Market celery is available throughout the year. Quite a lot comes from Florida in the USA, which seems a long way for it to have to travel.

It is best to eat the hearts uncooked, but the tougher stalks are very good braised or stewed in stock. Avoid if possible boiling in plain water as this rather ruins it. Celery, with its clear fresh taste, is one of those vegetables that, if you like it, can give a very special character to a recipe. Celery with carrots and apples is good for cooking with chicken or veal. Pigeon is very good cooked with celery, walnuts and smoked bacon.

Celery Braised

Clean and cut celery into 3-inch lengths and place in a saucepan or flameproof dish with 1—2 oz butter. Heat gently and once the cooking starts juices collect. A tablespoon of meat stock can be added. Season to taste. Cover and leave slowly cooking until the vegetable is tender (30 minutes).

Celery with Cheese

Braise the celery and when tender cover with sauce Mornay. Sprinkle with grated cheese and brown under a hot grill.

Alternatively, just sprinkle the celery with a mixture of 1 oz grated cheese and 1 oz bread crumbs, add a few drops of the cooking juices and brown under a hot grill.

Celery Fritters

Clean the celery, cut into one-inch pieces; dip these in a batter and fry in hot oil deep enough to just cover the pieces.

Drain on kitchen paper and serve immediately with some salt, or they are delicious eaten with sugar or honey.

BIDDY THE BASKET WOMAN

If ever you go to London town,
Just take a peep at Common Garden –
Market, I mean – there I'll be bound
You'll get your value to a farthing,
Of fruit and flowers, whate'er you wish,
You'll find it there – I tell you true, man –
Whate'er you choose, a dainty dish,
Brought home by Biddy the Basket Woman.

Wasn't I at Waterloo,
With a good canteen of whiskey too, man?
Few men did better their duty do,
Than Irish Biddy the Basket Woman!
When Mister Boney lost the sway,
Every man desarved his merits;
And I'm sure the glories of that day
Gave proof no soldier wanted spirits!

COURGETTES

With most varieties of marrow, the fruit can be picked while immature. Courgettes are baby marrows; they retain firm and delicious flesh which is lost as the vegetable grows big. The old jokey-giant vegetable marrow is dying out in England, and courgettes are being grown in their place. The French name, Courgette, is always used in England.

Courgettes have their knobbly ridge end sliced off and are then cooked unpeeled. Tiny ones can be cooked whole, and the larger ones are cut in half lengthways or sliced into rounds. They are cooked mixed with tomatoes and garlic or stewed, fried, battered or stuffed in much the same way as aubergines and, like aubergines, are better when cut, salted and left to drain for an hour or so before cooking.

Courgettes with Onion and Garlic

In Tavistock Street Luigi has a restaurant which is warm, friendly and Italian. It is one of the many houses that Nell Gwynne is said to have graced by a brief residence. A personal memory for Luigi is his mother cooking courgettes by chopping them coarsely and stewing them with onions in a little salted water with a whole clove of garlic and a sprinkling of rosemary. Cook until the liquid evaporates and the vegetables are soft but not brown. Diced potatoes can be cooked in the same way.

Stuffed Courgettes

All the stuffings suggested for aubergines are fine for courgettes and the method is the same but the courgettes need only about 20 minutes to cook.

Try using up any left-over ends of cheese, breadcrumbs, cooked aubergine, pepper, tomato, rice or meat reheated with the courgette flesh to make stuffing, but don't fill them too full.

Courgette Soufflé

Cook 1 lb of courgettes by boiling them whole in a little salted water. When tender drain and liquidize to a purée, then, if necessary, drain again by standing in a fine sieve. Make a mixture of 4 egg yolks, 1 heaped tablespoon of flour, 3 oz of butter, salt, pepper, a pinch of nutmeg and the courgette purée. Beat the 4 egg whites until stiff and fold into the mixture, turn into a buttered soufflé dish, and cook in a hot oven. When it is well risen and browned on top just leave to cook 5 minutes more and then it should not collapse. Eat immediately.

Right:
Market scene,
1747

Courgette Sticks

Cut courgettes into little strips like tiny chips. Salt them and leave them to drain for an hour. Rinse and dry them really well in a cloth. Fry them golden brown in deep enough fat; this only takes a minute or two.

Courgettes with Tomatoes and Mushrooms

Cut one large onion into slices and cook gently in a pan with an ounce of butter or olive oil. After a few minutes add a pound of courgettes cut into medium slices, salt, pepper, half a glass of wine, half a pound of peeled and chopped tomatoes and a quarter of a pound of sliced mushrooms. Simmer in an open saucepan until tender (7 minutes).

This has a more Mediterranean flavour when cooked with garlic and it then goes well with fish.

CRESS

In England, cress is always grown and sold with mustard. The tiny leaves of mustard and cress are served as a salad or to decorate other salads. It also makes excellent sandwiches. In the USA cress is known as small salad.

CUCUMBER

As cool as a cucumber and refreshing. Cucumbers have the right to be taken raw: in sandwiches, salads, yogurts and cold soups. If you wish to cook them, salt them, leave them to drain and then wash off the salt before cooking. This, I am sure, is intended for the recipe which follows.

Fried Cucumbers *(18th-century manuscript)*

"You must brown some butter in a pan, and pare and slice (but not too thin) six middling cucumbers. Drain them from the water, then put to them a little pepper and salt, a lump of butter, a spoonful of vinegar, a little shredded onion, a little gravy (not to make it too thin), and shake them well together with a little flour. You may lay these around your mutton as a sauce, or they are proper for a side dish."

Boiled Cucumber

If you wish, peel the cucumber. Cut it into cubes, moisten, add salt and cook gently in a covered pan until translucent and tender. Serve with Béchamel sauce.

ENDIVE

Total confusion is normal regarding the name of this vegetable. Is it endive or chicory? Old cook books in English call it witloof, a Flemish name, while fairly recent ones know it as chicory witloof or just chicory. In the Market it is most often called endive or Belgian endive. The use of the word endive (instead of chicory) probably comes from the USA.

What we are talking about is a slightly bitter-tasting, succulent salad vegetable with, broad, tightly packed, silvery leaves. It is a close relative of the chicory whose roots are roasted and ground to add to coffee. Grown under straw for warmth and to keep its sun-starved whiteness, besides making excellent salad it is a good vegetable to cook in winter.

When cooked, endive has a strong taste and goes well with cheese, veal, ham or chicken dishes.

Normally endive can be cooked as it is bought, with no preparation, although very fat ones may be best sliced once down the middle, particularly if they are to be cooked together with quite small ones.

Endives Baked with Ham

Beat 3 eggs into ¼ pint of cream, mix with a pint of milk and season with salt and pepper. If you like it less rich, you can use ½ pint of Béchamel or Mornay sauce. Take 4 endives, wrap each one in a slice of ham and tie up with a piece of cotton. Put the rolls into a casserole dish, cover with the egg mixture or sauce and bake in the top of a preheated moderate oven for 40 minutes. Grated cheese can be sprinkled over it.

Braised Endive

Lay the endives in a lightly buttered casserole dish or saucepan and add about ½ oz of butter for each; sprinkle with salt and pepper. Once the butter has started to sizzle, turn the heat down low, cover and leave to cook gently until the endives are tender (20–30 minutes). If left any longer, they may collapse. Before serving sprinkle with lemon juice.

    Small pieces of bacon can be cooked in the casserole until just brown and left to finish cooking with the endives. Done the same way in a moderate oven they take longer (1 hour).

FENNEL

The fennel in Covent Garden all comes from Italy, where two crops a year ensure that we are supplied during most months. It looks like a root, a bulbous form of celery, but is in fact an induced enlargement of the leaf stems at their base. Fennel tastes like aniseed. It should never be boiled. It is best stewed in meat stock. It can be prepared in practically every way suitable for celery. Fennel seeds come from a wilder, more stalky variety of fennel. Both sorts are shown on the opposite page.

Braised Fennel

Fennel braised with kipper fillets makes an excellent, unusual hors d'oeuvre. Slice ½ lb fennel into thin strips and fry it gently in oil. When nearly soft (½ hour) add four kipper fillets, cover and cook for 4 minutes. Serve hot.

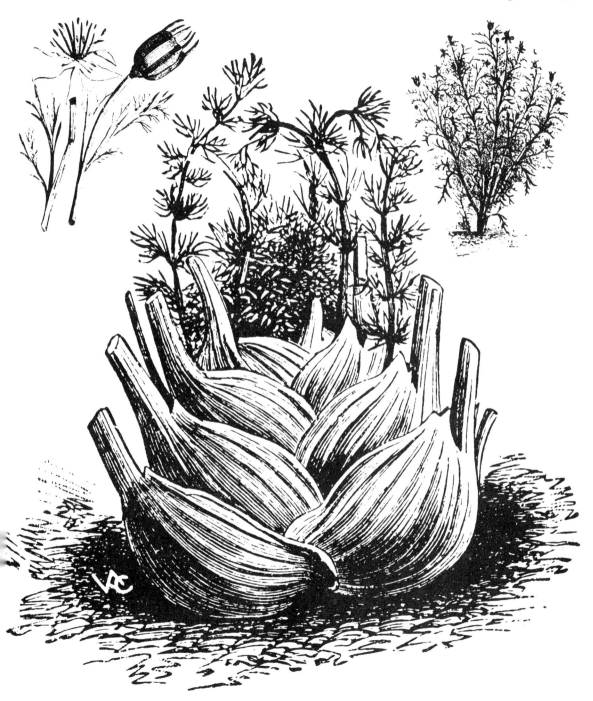

HORSERADISH

This is Marcel Boulestin's recipe for Horseradish sauce:

"Peel and chop very finely two small shallots, fry them in butter until brown; then add one ounce of grated horseradish, a tablespoonful of vinegar, some chopped parsley, salt and pepper. Cook slowly for ten minutes, after which add a claret glassful of cream. Cook it again till thoroughly hot, but do not bring it to the boil."

MARCEL BOULESTIN AND HIS RESTAURANT

Boulestin's restaurant in Southampton Street was reputedly the most expensive in London in the 1920s and yet still lost money. It was the height of fashion to dine at Boulestin's, surrounded by early Art Deco murals, fabrics and fitments in the spacious rooms of what was previously the Covent Garden, an Edwardian hotel built on the site of the Bedford Head Hotel ("When sharp with hunger, scorn you to be fed, Except on chick peas at the Bedford Head" — Alexander Pope).

Marcel Boulestin first came to England in the early 1920s and unlike many Frenchmen he found England pleasant and English food interesting. He returned to London in 1926 to found his restaurant. Pressure of finances turned his attention to culinary journalism and authorship, and he is said to have been the first to demonstrate cookery on television. The restaurant has changed little since his death in 1943 and is now managed by the charming Mr Willy. The present chef Mr Theron uses many original Boulestin recipes, a few of which can be found in this book.

Jerusalem Artichoke

This curious looking root was observed growing as a cultivated plant in Massachusetts in 1605. It was rapidly introduced to Europe under different names, but because its flavour is so similar to the globe artichoke, the name artichoke stuck. The word Jerusalem which in England was attached early on, probably before the Italians had given the plant the name Girasole, is most likely an anglicization of Ter Neusen, the place in Holland from where many specimens were distributed.

They are best scrubbed but not peeled, then steamed or cooked in very little salted water. When tender the skins can be rubbed off, and they can be served with butter or any white sauce, a cheese sauce being particularly suitable. The artichokes are simply reheated in the sauce and then, if required, browned under the grill.

Jerusalem Artichokes with Cheese *(from a 19th-century Sussex manuscript)*

"Boil two pounds of Jerusalem artichokes, drain, and mash them up with one gill of milk. (Mashed cooked onions are an improvement; and yesterday's onion sauce is an admirable substitute for milk.) Turn the mixture into a well-buttered baking dish, dust the top well with cheese, and bake till the top becomes coloured."

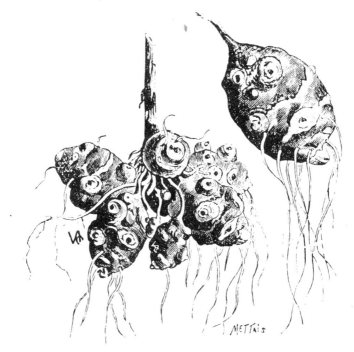

Kohl-Rabi

A cousin of the cabbage, kohl-rabi must be grown quickly and used when fresh. It can be cooked and served in the same ways as turnip. Since much of the flavour is in the skin, kohl-rabi tastes best when cooked unpeeled, either by steaming or in a very little salted water. Allowed to cool, it can be served sliced as salad with vinaigrette or mayonnaise, or with vinegar alone like beetroot.

LEEKS

"Eat leeks in lide rainson in may,
  Then all the year after physicians can play."
(lide = March, *rainson* = wild garlic).

"He ever sate uppermost at Apollo's feast that brought thither the greatest headed leek."
Dr Muffet, *Health's Improvement*, 1655.

Leek and Tomato Stew

This is a good hors d'oeuvre or winter vegetable. It is also good when eaten cold.

2 lbs leeks, 3 tomatoes, 2 cloves of garlic, parsley, olive oil, lemon juice, salt, Worcester sauce.

Warm up 4 tablespoons of olive oil in a frying pan or a heavy saucepan. Put in cleaned and cut leeks and season with salt and Worcester sauce. Fry them for half a minute on each side, turn down the heat and cook slowly for about 10 minutes. As soon as the leeks are cooked, take them out and put in the tomatoes, peeled and chopped, with the garlic and some parsley. Boil and stir for a couple of minutes, then pour the mixture over the leeks.

Braised Leeks

For 1 lb of leeks, melt 2 oz of butter in a thick pan, then add the leeks, cleaned and cut into 2 or 3 inch pieces. Season with salt and half a dozen dashes of Worcester sauce. Once they start to sizzle, turn and after half a minute lower the heat and cook gently (10 minutes). They are cooked when a fork easily goes into the more solid root end; they will absorb the butter and have a light golden colour.

Leeks with Cheese

Braise the leeks and when they are just tender sprinkle over them 2 oz grated cheese, and brown at the top of a hot oven or under a moderate grill.

Leeks with Cheese Sauce

Braise the leeks and make ¼ pint of Mornay sauce. Pour the sauce over the leeks, sprinkle 1 oz grated cheese on top and brown in a hot oven or under a grill (3 or 4 minutes).

Leek and Ham Tart

Chop the white parts of 2 lbs of leeks into inch pieces and cook them gently in 1 oz butter until just soft, then add 2 oz of diced ham. Line an 8-inch pie tin with pastry. Put the leeks and ham on the pastry. Beat together 3 egg yolks, ¼ pint of cream and ¼ pint of milk. Season to taste with salt and pepper, then pour the mixture over the leeks. Dot a little butter on top of the tart and cook in a medium hot oven until the egg mixture sets (30 minutes). Left over chicken can replace the ham. If you do not have or do not want to use meat, just leave it out and perhaps add cooked potatoes or carrots.

This dish is good hot or cold.

Leeks Stewed with Cider

Cider and leeks with the peppery tang of Worcester sauce make a pleasing, English combination. Braise the leeks, but do not put the salt in at the beginning. When the leeks have been cooking for 3 or 4 minutes and are really hot, pour over a wine glass of cider, let it boil and then turn it down to simmer. Add 2 tablespoons of meat stock together with some Worcester sauce, stir and check the seasoning. Cover to finish cooking (10 minutes more). Try wine instead of cider. With red wine the result is rather beautiful. If it is more convenient, finish off the cooking in a slow moderate oven (30 minutes).

Poireaux à la Niçoise

The restaurant named after Inigo Jones occupies a beautiful Victorian brick building on the corner of Floral Street and Garrick Street. Once a stained-glass window factory, the designers found that some glass had been left in the basement and this now decorates the walls, glistening through the cool gloom. Mr Santosh, the chef, is Austrian, although his name is of Portuguese origin; this is one of his recipes for leeks.

For 4 people:
   20 young leeks, 2 peeled tomatoes, a stick of celery with the top leaves, 2 carrots, ½ onion, 3 oz sour cream, 2 tablespoons mayonnaise, salt and pepper.
   Boil leeks in fond (stock or bouillon). Drain and leave to cool. Chop other ingredients finely and poach with white wine until this is reduced. Leave to cool, then mix with sour cream and mayonnaise and season to taste. Serve the leeks covered with the sauce.

Leek Roly-Poly

The most splendid figure in Covent Garden is, without doubt, Sergeant Major Vic Martin, commissionaire of the Royal Opera House. He is a man who obviously enjoys good food. He gave me this recipe with full military charm:
   "Make a good old-fashioned suet roly-poly and stir in some diced leek and chopped bacon. Serve it hot with any vegetable, or eat it cold. It is delightful, when cold, fried for breakfast. With any paste left over, mix into it figs or currants and then you have a sweet, commonly known as Spotted Dick."

For the Roly-Poly:
½ lb self-raising flour and 4 oz shredded suet mixed to a stiff dough with a little water or milk. Roll this to a sausage about 3 inches thick, wrap it in foil or a floured cloth and steam it for at least 45 minutes. Leaving it to cook for longer will do no harm.

THE ROYAL OPERA HOUSE COVENT GARDEN

Today the home of the Royal Opera Company and the Royal Ballet Company, the theatre was opened by John Rich in 1733 with a performance of Congreve's The Way of the World. *In its up-and-down history, the theatre was totally destroyed by fire in 1808, 1847 and 1856. E.M. Barry was the architect who designed the present theatre together with the adjoining Floral Hall, both of which opened in 1860.*

The Floral Hall, used for sales of home-grown flowers, was available during the winter months for concerts, dancing and even ice-skating. This arrangement ended abruptly one Saturday evening in 1865 as the audience was settling down for a concert, when a poster was displayed in the hall reading: "NOTICE TO VISITORS. The Committee regret to have to announce the receipt of a solicitor's letter from the Duke of Bedford ordering the immediate suppression of music. The concert, therefore, cannot take place."

The sculptor Flaxman, who was a resident of New Row, executed the statues and relief panels that ornament the facade of the theatre.

LETTUCE

"A dish of lettuce and a clear fountain can cool all my heat."

Jeremy Taylor, 1651.

"Because lettuces are owned by the moon they cool and moisten what heat and dryness Mars causeth. The juice of the lettuce mixed or boyled with oil of roses and applied to the forehead and temples, procureth sleep and easeth the Head-ache procceeding of an hot cause."

Culpeper, *Herbal*, 1653.

Boiled Lettuce

A good idea if there is a glut is to try cooking lettuce, any type of lettuce, including the curly endive. Wash the lettuce and put it into a little boiling salted water. As lettuces reduce like spinach to surprisingly little, a small lettuce per person is a fair helping. Boil until tender (5 minutes) then strain thoroughly and chop them up. Melt 2 oz of butter in a saucepan and add the lettuce, sprinkle on a teaspoon of flour for each lettuce, some lemon juice and simmer gently until ready (10 minutes). Nutmeg can be used as a spice.

An alternative method is to omit the lemon juice, instead adding a tablespoon of cream and stirring in two egg yolks before serving.

Cooked lettuce, like spinach, makes a bed for poached eggs. It can be served with fish or cheese sauce, or with chicken or veal in Béchamel or Mornay sauce.

Lettuce Braised with Bacon

In a large frying pan, with 1 oz of butter, cook until tender 4 slices of streaky bacon cut into thin strips, one onion chopped fine and one carrot chopped very fine. Put 4 heads of lettuce into a little salted, boiling water for 5 minutes, remove and drain thoroughly, squeeze in a colander, then mould the wilted leaves into four fat squares in the middle of the frying pan and spoon some of the bacon mixture over them. Pour over enough stock or bouillon to cover the lettuce (about ½ pint), sprinkle with thyme, cover the pan and simmer (¾ hour) or put in a low oven (1½ hours). Sprinkle with parsley before serving.

"The first and foremost place of all kinds of lettuce is the salad bowl."
André Simon's *Concise Encyclopaedia of Gastronomy*, 1941

MARROW

Marrow in Tomato Sauce with Cheese *(from Mrs Eve Patrick who lives in Drury Lane)*

2-3 lbs of marrow are cut into cubes and simmered in stock for 10 minutes. Mix the marrow in some tomato sauce and turn the mixture into a buttered ovenproof dish. Slice a small packet of cream cheese into thin slices and spread these over. Cover the top with grated cheese and bake in a hot oven for 30 minutes.

Marrow in White Sauce

Wash and scrape a marrow and grate it into a colander. Sprinkle liberally with salt and leave to stand until a lot of juice has run out (1 hour). Wash out the salt and brine in cold water and sweat the marrow over a low heat with enough butter to prevent it sticking. When it becomes soft enough to eat, but still a little crisp, sift on about the same amount of flour as the butter used. When the flour has been cooked for a few minutes stir in hot milk and heat gently, stirring continuously until the sauce just runs off the spoon. Adjust the seasoning, add a pinch of nutmeg, and continue cooking until the floury taste has gone (5 minutes).

Braised Marrow *(Chinese)*

Peel and seed 1 lb of marrow, cut it into small cubes and fry until golden in 1 tablespoon of oil. Season with salt, pepper and ground ginger, add 1 dessertspoon of cornflour diluted with enough cold water or cider to make a thin cream, and simmer until soft (8 minutes). Sprinkle with finely chopped spring onions before serving.

Stuffed Marrow *(18th-century Sussex recipe)*

A marrow about 2 lbs weight, an onion, ½ teaspoon mixed herbs, ½ lb minced or finely chopped meat, cooked or raw or sausage meat, 1 oz of butter or oil, salt and pepper.

Chop the onion finely and fry it slowly until golden brown, add the meat, herbs, salt, pepper and stir together over the heat. Cut about one inch off the end of the marrow, the flower end not the stalk end. With a sharp knife, hollow out the centre flesh to remove the seeds and the pithy threads holding them. (The dried seeds can be eaten like nuts.) Thrust the stuffing into the cavity, replace the end as a lid and tie it in place. Cook in a preheated medium oven for about an hour.

MUSHROOMS

Borrow at least £80,000 from a friend, join the Mushroom Growers Association, equip your specially designed, ventilated, heated sheds according to the special know-how of the MGA and from the time the spores have run, which is eleven days, to the time when the mushrooms are in their boxes ready for the market, it will be four to six weeks. Any time of the year, rain or shine but only one variety: the Agaricus Bisporus. In other lands chanterelles, ceps and a host of other fungi are eaten with delight but here we are in business, in a highly specialised industry and neither the public nor the grower is likely to bite off anything other than a "button", a "cap", or an "open" unless someone is prepared to risk a lot more money getting people to unlearn what their grandmother taught them about toadstools.

As for eating mushrooms, they offer practically no calories but some vitamins, minerals and a suspicion of protein. There is no need to peel them and they can be taken raw in salads. Cook them covered, gently, and try to arrange to serve them from the very same pot they were cooked in.

Grilled Mushrooms

"Mushrooms are found abundantly throughout Shetland; they form a wholesome and appetising food. Wipe, remove stalk and peel; dip in egg and breadcrumbs and fry a golden brown in enough fat almost to cover."

This recipe comes from *The Shetland Cookery Book* by Margaret B. Stout and I found it in The Scottish Merchant, a shop in New Row full of lovely Fair-Isle and Shetland sweaters, shawls and other Scottish cottage-industry goods.

Carefully clean the mushrooms and put them, hollow side up, in a buttered baking tray or grill pan; fill the cavities with butter and sprinkle them all with salt and freshly-ground pepper. Grill them gently for about 10 minutes.

It may be convenient to have the mushrooms prepared beforehand and then cook them in an oven. At the top of a preheated moderate oven, they will take about 12 minutes.

Mushrooms with Parsley and Garlic

Gently fry some mushrooms in oil for 3 minutes, then add for each ½ lb of mushrooms 1 clove of garlic, 2 tablespoons of parsley, salt and freshly-ground black pepper. Cover the pan and cook slowly (15 minutes).

A teaspoon of chopped fresh mint instead of the parsley makes a refreshing change.

Mushrooms à la Grecque

This is a simple version of the classic dish:

4 tablespoons olive oil
3 shallots or spring onions or one
  chopped onion
1 crushed clove of garlic
¼ pint dry white wine
1 lb mushrooms
4 peeled and seeded tomatoes cut in
  half crossways; squeeze each half
  gently through a sieve

2 tablespoons chopped parsley
1 small stick of celery chopped very
  fine
1 sprig of fennel sliced very fine
1/8 teaspoon chopped thyme
juice of half a lemon
salt
freshly ground black pepper

Heat the oil and fry the onion and garlic first until they are soft. Then stir in the wine and all the other ingredients except the parsley. Cook gently for about 13 minutes. Chill. Just before serving stir in the parsley.

You can make this without the tomatoes or with a pinch of ground cloves.

Mushrooms with Butter and Milk

¼ lb of mushrooms are wiped clean and may be sliced if they are too big. This recipe only works well if most of the mushrooms are in one layer. Melt some butter in a saucepan, about 1 oz per ¼ lb and put in the mushrooms. Once warmed up over a moderate heat pour in a coffee cup of milk; this boils quickly. Turn the heat down, sprinkle with salt and pepper, put a lid on the pan and allow to simmer for 10 minutes, shaking it around once or twice.

Mushrooms Provençale

1 lb mushrooms, 2 tablespoons olive oil, 2 tablespoons chopped parsley, 1 clove garlic, ¼ pint white wine, 1½ tablespoons flour.

If the mushrooms are large, quarter them; if small leave whole. Heat the oil in a frying pan, add the mushrooms, parsley and the garlic crushed. Fry gently for 8 minutes, stirring occasionally. Sprinkle on the flour and stir it gently, leave to cook for 1 minute and then blend in the wine, 2 tablespoons of water or stock, salt and pepper to taste. Bring just to the boil and simmer gently until ready (10 minutes).

Stuffed Mushrooms

Choose the largest mushrooms you can find that are still slightly bowl-shaped. Wipe them clean and remove the stalks. For 1 lb mushrooms, chop 2 oz ham or bacon, a tablespoon of parsley, 1 clove of garlic and the mushroom stalks. Mix these ingredients with 1 oz grated parmesan cheese and 1 oz breadcrumbs and season well. Put the mushrooms on an oiled baking tray and gently fill them with the mixture. Pour a little olive oil onto each mushroom. Cook at the top of a moderate oven for about half an hour. If they tend to dry up put more oil on them. The anchovy meat stuffings used with aubergines are also good with mushrooms.

"On Tuesday, three men named Edward Barton, John Cripps and John Tomlin, were convicted under the Covent-garden Market Act, in penalties of 10s. each, for having created a disturbance in that market. Barton and Cripps were, in addition, sentenced to three months' imprisonment and hard labour, for having indecently exposed their persons."
Newspaper report, 2 September 1834

OKRA

Okra or ladies' fingers are good stewed with onions and tomatoes. The dish is called Bamyes in Greece.

Trim the tops from a pound of okra, wash and spread out on a dish, sprinkle with salt and after an hour wash off any slime. In the meantime slice 2 onions and half a pound of tomatoes and stew them slowly with a little olive oil and a little water. When the okra is ready put it into this sauce, add some salt and pepper, a teaspoonful of sugar and a teaspoonful of vinegar. Bring gently to the boil and cook slowly for about an hour. This vegetable then improves in flavour if it is left to stand until tepid or cold before serving.

ONIONS

"Onions sodden in milk, when eaten salad wise with sweet oil, vinegar and sugar are hurtful to no person nor complexions."

Dr Muffet, *Health's Improvement*, 1655.

This key vegetable has a wonderful and widespread reputation for health, to purify the blood and for building the body. Sufficient onion in the diet to build a wonderful physique may be dreadfully destructive socially.

"Let onion atoms lark within the bowl
And, scarce suspected, animate the whole."

This was the Rev. Sydney Smith's (1771-1845) advice and it can be read as a lesson in etiquette as well as the culinary art. However, when the very best onions are available it is worth ignoring this caution in order to eat them cooked whole or generously chopped into salads.

In the Market, English onions are rated the best; they start in September and are finished by the end of April. Spanish are rated next best and start when the English finish. When English or Spanish are difficult to get there are often Dutch onions or they even come from as far as Chile or Egypt, but these are probably the ones to use sparingly.

In old cookery books a scallion is often called for; this is the ciboule, a small leek-like onion and actually of Siberian origin though often called a Welsh onion.

Spring Onions

A spring onion is a seedling onion, and is in the market during all seasons. In bad weather they come from Italy. They are mostly eaten raw in salads. The best cooks in the world, the Chinese, however, use them in preference to other cooking onions. Try frying chopped spring onions with a few fennel leaves as an accompaniment to veal or fish.

Shallot

The name is a corruption of the word Ascalon, an area of Palestine, where this small onion originated. It was introduced into England in 1548 and has a milder flavour than the onion. Its bulbs divide like garlic into "cloves". It is highly thought of in French recipes.

Beurre Marchand de Vins

Shallot butter with red wine, to top steaks, hamburgers or liver. 1 tablespoon of chopped

shallots are boiled with ⅛ pint of red wine, a tablespoon of beef bouillon or meat glaze and some pepper.

When only one third of the mixture is left, set it aside to cool. With a fork, cream 4 oz butter, then beat it a little at a time into the wine mixture. Finally beat in a good handful of chopped parsley and check the seasoning.

Pissaladière

Bread dough (wholemeal flour and salt mixed with water and left in a warm place to rise a little will do), 2 small black olives, 1 clove, 3 filleted anchovies, lots of onions, olive oil, 1 clove garlic, a little salt, 1 bay leaf.

Cut the onions into strips and fry them slowly in the olive oil with the clove, chopped garlic, and the bay leaf. Line a baking tray with the bread dough. Spread thickly with the onions, pepper well, add just a speck of salt and dot with olives and anchovies. Bake in a brisk oven for about 15 minutes.

Serve very hot, cut in strips.

White Glazed Onions

This dish looks best with small onions, 1½ inches or less in diameter, peeled and left whole. If only big ones are available, peel and slice them. Put the onions in a frying pan or a heavy saucepan large enough to take them in one layer. Pour over ¼ pint of white stock, white wine, water or a mixture of any of these. Add 1 oz butter, salt, pepper and a simple bouquet garni. Simmer very gently for 40–50 minutes, moving them about from time to time. The onions should not colour. Onions cooked in this way are good served with parsley.

Stuffed Onions

4 large onions, ¼ lb sausage meat, ¼ lb minced beef, 2 oz butter, 2 tablespoons flour, ½ pint bouillon or stock, 1 teaspoon brandy or sherry, salt and pepper and a teaspoonful of thyme.

Peel the onions and with a sharp knife cut in half and then around in order to scoop out their centres: rather like preparing a grapefruit. Slice these centres very finely and brown in butter. Sprinkle on the flour, mix in well and cook for a minute before adding the stock, brandy, salt and pepper. Fill the onions with a mixture of the two meats and the thyme. Put them into a baking dish or casserole and pour the sauce over. Cook for 1½–2 hours in a moderate oven. Spoon the sauce over the onions several times during the cooking.

Baked Onions

Put 4 large onions, with their skins on, in a baking tray, into a slow oven for 1½–2 hours. Serve them hot in their skins with butter or salt and pepper or a vinaigrette dressing. Big pink-fleshed Spanish onions can take 2½ hours to cook.

Brown Braised Onions

Heat 1 oz of butter or oil in a frying pan or heavy saucepan. Fry the onions until as evenly browned as possible. Add ¼ pint brown stock, beef bouillon, wine or water, salt, pepper and a bouquet garni or a sprinkling of thyme. Cover and simmer gently until the stock is absorbed leaving the onions glowing, brown and tender (¾ hour).

The same result can be achieved by putting the onions, once they have been fried and covered with the liquid, into a dish and cooking, uncovered, in the oven.

Onions in Cream Sauce

Make ½ pint of Béchamel sauce, pour it over glazed onions and allow the two to simmer together for 5 minutes.

Onions Stewed in Wine or Cider

Peel onions, all of the same size, and fry them lightly with a tablespoon of oil. Pour over them a glass of wine or cider. Sprinkle with salt and pepper and once the liquid has boiled for a minute, add water to a level halfway up the onions and transfer to a low oven for about 1½ hours. If the wine sauce is too runny reduce it by boiling briskly and pour over the onions before serving.

Fried Onion Rings

Slice large onions and divide into rings. Dip the rings in milk and then in flour. Fry them in very hot oil. As soon as they are golden and crips drain them and serve them hot with salt.

PARSNIPS

"And the roote of the parsnep hanged on the necke, doth helpe the swelling of the throte: and no venemous worme shall harme the person which beareth the root about him!"

Old saying.

Parsnips fried to look like Trout *(from a Yorkshire manuscript dated 1769)*

"Take a middling sort of parsnips, not overthick and boil them as soft as you would do for eating; peel and cut them in two the long way. You must only fry the small ends not the thick ones. Beat two or three eggs; put to them a tablespoon of flour, dip in your parsnips and fry them a light brown in butter. Have for your sauce, a little vinegar and butter."

Parsnip Chips

Scrub the parsnips and peel them if the skins are rough or tough, then slice the vegetables into tiny stick chips. Fry in hot oil till just golden brown; this only takes a minute. Dry on kitchen paper and serve with salt.

Parsnip Purée

Clean the parsnips then put them into boiling, salted water and simmer gently until tender. Skin them and mash them, finish with pepper, milk, cream and butter in a liquidizer or push them through a sieve.

This makes a good sauce for cod.

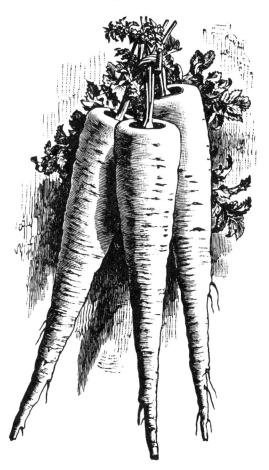

PEAS

Because peas look so pleasing and are a good accompaniment to almost anything from a humble fried egg to elaborately prepared meat, they are the most popular vegetable after the potato. It is, however, possible that at least part of their popularity is due to the fact that they freeze and tin so well and have become a very hard-sold commodity. This should make it even more of a treat to have fresh peas but they must be well cooked and so I have given one recipe each for French-style peas, for small tender young peas, for large tender peas and for the big toughies.

Peas used to be shelled in Covent Garden and sold by the pint, gallon, peck and bushel (1 bushel = 4 pecks = 8 gallons = 64 pints). 1 lb of small tender young peas gives about ½ lb when shelled, allowing helpings for between one and three people, depending on appetites and the meal. 1 lb of large peas gives more when shelled, something like ¾ lb.

Peas with Onions *(for large but still tender peas)*

1 lb peas, 6 shallots or small onions, 1 dessertspoon sugar, 1½ oz butter, 1 chopped mint leaf.

Chop the shallots and boil them with the peas for about 10 minutes until they are almost, but not quite, cooked enough to eat. Drain them. Melt the butter in a saucepan, put in the peas and shallots, sprinkle with the sugar, chopped mint, salt, pepper, and cook covered over a low heat occasionally tossing until they are tender.

Peas with Ham *(for young tender peas)*

2 lbs peas, 1 small onion, 1 oz butter and 3 oz cooked ham cut into strips.

Soften the onion in the butter, put in the shelled peas and a dessertspoonful of water, cook this gently and after 5 minutes add the ham. After a further 5–10 minutes the peas should be ready and the liquid evaporated. Sprinkle with salt and pepper and serve, perhaps as an hors d'oeuvre.

Buttered Peas *(for larger tougher green peas)*

1 lb peas, 1 head of lettuce chopped fine, ½ dessertspoonful of sugar, 2 chopped shallots or small onions, 1½ oz of butter, salt and pepper.

Put all the ingredients into a saucepan and just cover them with cold water. Cover the pan and boil for about 20 minutes or until the peas are tender. The liquid should have been absorbed and evaporated, but add more if required. Any excess can be reduced by boiling with the lid off.

Jugged Peas

This 18th-century recipe from Surrey is one of the best ways to cook peas at any time during the season.

"Shell a pint of peas, put them into a clean two-pound pickle bottle or any jar with a closely fitting top, adding a tablespoon of butter, a teaspoon of powdered sugar, a salt-spoon of salt, a dozen mint leaves, and at discretion, a very little black pepper. Cover

Mary, queen of the pea shellers, enthroned on the left. For 56 years she amazed onlookers by the speed of her work (1912)

the vessel tightly and immerse it to the extent of half its depth in a pan of boiling water. Set the latter on the fire and boil briskly. Examine in half an hour; the peas if very young should be done by then, if old they will of course take longer."

Buttered Peas *(for fresh, young, tender peas)*

Shell the peas and put them into boiling salted water, boil gently with the saucepan uncovered until they are just tender. This need only take 4 minutes. Strain them in a colander. Turn into a heated dish and dot with butter.

Buttered Peas *(for larger but tender green peas)*

Put the peas into boiling water with a sprig of mint in it if you like the flavour. When they are very nearly tender enough to eat (between 5 and 10 minutes), drain them. Melt 1 oz butter for each 1 lb peas, into a saucepan, put the peas into this with a teaspoon of sugar and some pepper. Cover the pan and roll and toss the peas occasionally; leave the heat low until the peas are ready to eat. This will take something like 10 minutes.

A la Française

Giovanni's restaurant in Goodwin Court recommends this as the ultimate in pea cookery, but claims it for the Italians by calling it "piselli Francese". Any peas, including tinned peas, are improved by cooking them with onions, but if you have good fresh peas, spring onions and a head of lettuce and cook them together as below, then you will have a dish to be taken seriously and eaten separately with a spoon.

2 oz butter, with ¼ pint of water, salt, pepper and a little sugar are brought to the boil and a pound of shelled peas are tossed in. Put some parsley in with the peas, tied with a string so it can be removed when the cooking is complete. Quarter a lettuce lengthways and arrange the quarters on top of the peas. The lettuce quarters may be parcelled with string to prevent disintegration. Scatter about a dozen spring onion bulbs over the lettuce and cover the saucepan with a plate or soup dish so that the evaporated cooking liquor mainly drops back into the saucepan. Ideally when the cooking is complete (20 minutes) the cooking liquid will have evaporated. The peas can be tossed with a little more butter before serving and the lettuce quarters arranged around the edge of the dish.

Purée of Peas

"Have your peas cooked in half wine, half water. When they are tender add the crumb of white bread and cook together. Then let the peas cool. Put them through a sieve with clarified butter and do not forget to sweeten them if you want to. Some do not."

Le Grand Cuisinier de Toute Cuisine, dated 1350.

PEPPERS

Three members of the Capsicum family regularly make the journey to the Market. In popular appeal the head of the family is the capsicum himself, a tomato-like object, usually quite large, and green, golden or red according to age. This capsicum is known as a pepper, pimento or, perhaps because paprika is made from the seeds, as paprika capsicum. Coming from Holland or England, eaten cooked or raw, the capsicum is nowadays found in almost every greengrocer's. The cousins are less popular: the small hot pepper or chili, used in Indian and Greek restaurants, ground up makes cayenne pepper. It has a large relative, the sweet or salad pepper which is almost identical in appearance but usually at least twice the size.

Peperonata

4 red peppers, 5 tomatoes, a small onion, 1 clove garlic, butter and oil.

Take the peppers with seeds and stalks removed, and the onions and cut into fine strips. Chop the garlic fine. Fry all these together in a mixture of half butter and half oil. When tender turn the heat down and allow to simmer for a quarter of an hour. Peel and chop the tomatoes and add these to the pan. Simmer for half an hour, allowing the liquid from the tomatoes to evaporate. The mixture should be coated but not swimming or sitting in oil. It can be served hot or cold.

Peppers Stewed with Tomatoes

Cut 2 large red or green peppers in half and remove all the seeds and the stalks. Cut them into thin strips. Heat a tablespoon of olive oil (or use cheaper oil mixed with some olive oil) in a frying pan; gently fry the pepper strips. Add a chopped clove of garlic, cover and leave for 10 minutes. Skin and chop one lb of tomatoes, add these to the pan and sprinkle with basil, salt and pepper. Stir and cook the mixture until the liquid thickens to a sauce. Good with food that traditionally has cooked tomatoes served with it in restaurants; for example egg dishes, sausages, grills and fried liver.

Stuffed Peppers

If the peppers will stand easily on end just cut the lids off and remove the seeds. If they insist on lying down, cut them in half lengthways. Take out the stalks and seeds and fill with any stuffing suggested for aubergines or courgettes. Brush them with oil and put them into an oiled tray or dish that can be covered and put into a low oven for an hour. Check that they do not dry up, basting them as required.

POTATOES

" . . . . Public markets do not require hard or soft sells to induce their clients to use them."

Ivan Illich, *Deschooling Society.*

For upwards of three hundred years, people have gathered at Covent Garden to buy produce from fields and gardens for resale on the stalls in the market. A lot of business today is negotiated person to person, on the telephone, between the stall holder and the growers. Some products, mushrooms and watercress, for example, are grown under special conditions that lead growers to group together in trade associations. These voluntary associations may levy their members for funds and impose their own standards on members and the products they offer to the market. They may also try to bend the iron laws of supply and demand to their members' advantage. However there is no compulsion by law to join, to pay up, or to remain a member just because you grow and sell watercress, mushrooms or whatever. Apples and pears are something else, however, for by Act of Parliament the Apple and Pear Development Council may levy growers for funds for its work.

Quite different indeed is the potato, for here the law of the land has set up a Potato Marketing Board with a statutory duty to regulate the production of a suitable quantity of potatoes each year. Anyone growing more than one acre must register with the Board and the potato crop may only be sold to registered dealers. Recent figures show that the average UK consumption of potatoes is 220 lbs per person per year and at a price around 50p a bag (of 56 lbs), growers are selling nearly £100 million worth of potatoes a year. This considerable business is regulated by a levy system, ingeniously permissive, which has enabled the Board to operate without much interference at the point of sale. Each grower has a registered acreage and in any year may grow a quota of that acreage (say 90 per cent) for a standard levy (£4—£5 per acre in recent years). If the grower decides to plant more than his quota he pays a much higher levy (about £25 per acre) on each acre in excess of his quota. If potatoes drop in price below a pre-determined level the Board buys in potatoes to support the price and then resells (probably at a loss) potatoes for animal feed.

Generally the Board has not advertised much and has only gently urged standardizing and institutionalizing the 'marketing' side. Perhaps the low profile maintained explains the seemingly charmed existence of the Board which was established in 1934. The Cucumber and Tomato Marketing Board, a more pushy affair, was dissolved without much lament in the sixties.

Whether the Board can continue to play the game with new European rules is perhaps uncertain, in the meantime the Board will come more into the public gaze. A vigorous campaign to acquaint housewives with minimum standards of size and quality is on the launch pad and greengrocers are to have their arms gently twisted to persuade them to identify the potatoes on sale more exactly, not just as "reds" or "whites" but by the actual names of the varieties. Most of those who sell potatoes at Covent Garden show no interest in labelling their potatoes exactly.

"A food, also a meate . . . rosted in the embers, or boiled and eaten with oile, vinegar and pepper, or dressed any other way by the hand of someone cunning in cookerie."
Gerard's *Herball*, 1597

Probably brought back in about 1550 by Spaniards from South America where it was in regular cultivation and use, the potato spread from Spain throughout Europe. Sir John Hawkins, sometimes credited with the discovery, found the sweet potato, not the ordinary white potato. There is a story that in 1585 Sir Walter Raleigh brought potatoes from Virginia; however they were not known to have been grown there until the beginning of the 18th century. Sir Francis Drake's claim is supported by a monument in Germany dubbing him "Introducer of the potato into Europe in the year of Our Lord 1580."

Potatoes became popular in England during the 18th Century. In 1789 Gilbert White says they "are much esteemed here now by the poor". Early recipes often recommend cooking in their skins—good advice to this day.

"Potade roots engender much flesh" according to Dr Muffet's *Health's Improvement*, published in 1655.

Nowadays, the potato takes its place as one of the world's staple food crops. It is a stem tuber, a swollen underground food store for the plant, not a true root like a parsnip or a carrot. The stored food is mainly starch, which may constitute up to a quarter of the total weight. There is very little of the potato which, when cooked, is not digested, since the proportion of fibrous, unavailable carbohydrate is only about 1 per cent of the total weight. This, together with its family connections with the deadly nightshade, may account for its very high "yin" rating in the minds of those who believe "you are what you eat". Undoubtedly the potato is a major food for the English, often supplying one-third of the vitamin C intake. Calculation shows that eating 6½ lbs of boiled potatoes daily would supply 2,600 calories and enough nitrogen to prevent loss of bodily protein together with a fair supply of other minerals and vitamins. This calculation probably shows that the potato does not fully deserve its deadly reputation as a spreader of waist-lines, especially when eaten without extra fat, and indeed it can feature in slimming diets.

Recently, in the United Kingdom, a statistical connection was made between the incidence of *spina bifida*, a crippling condition of the newborn, and the consumption of blighted potatoes. No substance has been identified as the causal link and the statistical

results have not been obtained in comparable studies in Australia, so the matter is by no means proven. The possibility raised should be enough, however, to make one select potatoes carefully, and reject the nasties, preferably before they even reach the shopping basket.

Potato Pye

"Scald them well and pill them; then put butter into your pye, then whole mace, the Potatoes with Marrow, Cinnamon, Mace and sugar, then butter, so close it, and bake it, and when it is baked, put in some white wine, Butter and sugar, with yolks of eggs."

17th-century recipe.

New potatoes appear in the Market as early as February, the first, arriving from Cyprus and the Mediterranean. Since they are the better for being quite fresh the real pleasure of the new potatoes comes with the home crop, beginning in May. In June the second favourite, the Home Guard variety, arrives followed by Maris Peer which is available throughout the summer months. New potatoes, especially the Maris Peer, are very good for boiling, roasting, in salads or fried. They are not usually much good for baking or mashing. The first new potatoes are often good enough to need no more than boiling or cooking slowly in butter, they need no herbs to set them off. Use good fat such as butter, good dripping, olive oil or sunflower seed oil since they may absorb a good deal of whatever they are in. Later potatoes are improved with herbs, mint for boiling, garlic or rosemary when sautéed, or in casserole, or with meat, and, with chives or spring onion tops in salads. New potatoes should be put into boiling water with about one teaspoon of salt for each pound of potatoes.

The King Edward, red variety, is probably the favourite potato in the Market and is judged excellent for boiling, mashing, baking or roasting. It is good for frying as chips and can be used in salads. Of the whites, Pentland Crown is grown in greatest quantity and it has good qualities all round. Potatoes of all varieties are often described as having a mild flavour or a pleasant flavour. Since this means they do not taste of anything much they are particularly suitable objects on which to practise the arts of cookery. Overall hints are to buy good ones, to store them carefully in the dark (or they turn green), away from strong smells, to peel them thinly or not at all, not to keep them hot after cooking (better to reheat if necessary), to add a little lemon juice or vinegar when cooking, especially if they tend to blacken and to cook them quickly but not too much. Hard water is better than soft water for boiling potatoes.

A potato is cooked when its middle portion reaches 96° C for boiled potatoes and 98° C for baked potatoes. The cooking time therefore depends on size; one ounce pieces of potato (i.e. 16 pieces to a pound) take about 12 minutes to cook by boiling and four ounce pieces (i.e. four pieces to the pound) take about half an hour.

Tiny New Potatoes Cooked in Butter

Choose very small new potatoes and cut any longer ones in half. Scrub clean and dry. Melt ¼ lb of butter in a frying pan and cook the potatoes slowly. Turn them fairly often. The potatoes should be golden brown all over (30—40 minutes). Do not let the butter burn.

Latkes

Finely grate 4 peeled potatoes and one onion and leave standing in a colander for twenty minutes to drain the water off the potatoes. Mix with an egg, salt and pepper and fry dollops in a heavy pan with a quarter of an inch of oil, flattening them out and turning them as they cook. If the mixture seems too sloppy stir in a spoonful of flour. Juniper berries can be added as an unusual seasoning.

Browned Potatoes with Cheese *(19th-century recipe from Surrey)*

"Boil some potatoes in their 'jackets', but do not let them fall to pieces. Remove peel and pare them until they are all the same size. Have a little butter melted in a bowl, dip them in this, then roll them in grated cheese, seasoned with pepper and salt. Put them in a buttered tin in a good oven, when the cheese has coloured, serve 'hot and hot'."

Bubble and Squeak

Potatoes mashed with butter or dripping, but no milk, together with cabbage or Brussels sprouts are browned in a frying pan with dripping. Alternatively they can be made into cakes dusted with flour browned in a pan individually. Sometimes described as Rumbledethumps, it is a close English cousin of Cabbilow, which is browned in the oven, or of Kailcannon from the Celtic fringe where, alas, it may not be browned at all.

Potato Casserole

This is a savoury casserole to eat with fish or grilled or roasted meat.

2 lbs potatoes, 1 onion, 1 lb tomatoes, 6 anchovies, 2 tablespoons olive oil, 2 cloves garlic, ¼ teaspoon basil, ¼ teaspoon thyme, 1 oz grated cheese, salt and pepper.

Slice the onions and cook them slowly in half the oil. Peel the tomatoes and slice them into the onions, sprinkle with salt, stir and remove from the heat.

Mash into a paste the remaining oil with the anchovies, garlic, herbs and pepper. Make a layer of the tomato and onion mixture at the bottom of a casserole dish with a layer of the potatoes finely sliced on top, followed by some of the anchovy paste. Repeat the layers to finish with the tomato and onion on top. Sprinkle with cheese and a little oil and bake in a pre-heated medium oven until the potatoes are tender and the top is just beginning to brown (40 minutes).

Roast Potatoes

Potatoes can be roasted around a joint of meat. They will all be ready together if they are all about the same size. Baste occasionally during cooking and turn at least once.

Potatoes can be roasted more quickly and surely if they are almost cooked by boiling beforehand. If they are to be done on their own, put some oil or melted dripping in a tray and cook as before until well browned (40 minutes). The same method works well if the parboiled potatoes are cut into thick slices or large cubes. A few sprigs of rosemary can be laid on the potatoes before putting in the oven.

Potato Pie

Cool, cooked potatoes, mashed, and mixed to something thick and creamy with Mornay sauce, are put in a pie dish. Dot the top with butter, pepper too if you wish, and cook in a hot oven until the top browns.

Rösti

This is a Swiss recipe. Boil 1 lb of potatoes in their jackets but stop them cooking when they are still firm. Cool until you can peel them (a fork is helpful for holding hot potatoes) and grate coarsely. Finely chop a large onion and mix it with the potato and some salt and pepper. Heat 2 oz of butter in a frying pan. When the fat is really hot put in the potato mixture and press it down with a spatula so that the bottom of the pan is completely covered with a firm layer. Turn down the heat and leave to brown on the underside (10 minutes). The rösti has then to be turned over as a complete cake (you can invert it onto a large plate) in order to brown the other side (further 10 minutes).

The Swiss eat this with eggs.

Mashed Potatoes

Boil one pound of potatoes in a little water, drain and allow to dry. Mash them thoroughly, stir in an ounce of butter, seasoning and ¼ cup of hot milk. Whisk until light and slightly stiff. Crushed garlic can be added with the milk. Meat fat and juices from a roast can be used as well as butter and milk. When ready they should be eaten as soon as possible, as they tend to toughen up if kept hot.

Market scene, 1871

Boiled New Potatoes

After cleaning them with a brush, put them into boiling salted water and boil until just tender. Drain and serve with butter.

Potatoes in a Paper Bag

"No patent stove, no patent oven or apparatus of any kind are required. All that is necessary is an oven, a grid, and the paper bag . . . . When in the homes of modest resource the contents of the Paper Bag that has passed through the culinary process are placed upon the table, and the savoury smell has been succeeded by the delicious flavour, husband and children will join in the cry of homage to the new method of the ménagère, and exclaim: 'Oh, mother, now we know what cooking is!' "
Nicholas Soyer, *Soyer's Paper-Bag Cookery*, 1911.

Here are two of Soyer's recipes for potatoes. They work well using greaseproof bags:
New Potatoes - Peel, halve and put sufficient into a paper bag for three persons with three tablespoonfuls of cold water. Add one leaf of mint, and a little salt. Seal up the bag. Place gently on the grid. Allow 30—35 minutes in hot oven. All potatoes should be cut in two.
Pommes Paysanne - Cut half a dozen good-sized peeled potatoes into large dice; blanch for a minute or so. Place in a paper bag and add a chopped onion, four ounces of ham finely diced and two ounces of butter. Seal up and bake for 30 minutes.

Baked Potatoes

Scrub some fairly large potatoes with a scourer or stiff brush to remove any loose dirt, rub with salt and bake in a hot oven until soft when squeezed (1-1½ hours). It is convenient to choose potatoes of roughly the same size as they will all be ready at the same time. There is a perfection method, which I confess I have never had the opportunity to try out, where the potatoes are embedded in a tray of rock salt which can be re-used many times for the same purpose. This is said to leave the skins very crisp. Rock salt in quantity seems very difficult to obtain.

Stuffed Baked Potatoes

From a baked potato cut a piece from the flat side and scoop out the inside. Alternatively the potato can be cut in half lengthways. The cooked flesh can be mixed with salt, pepper, butter or cream-cheese and the following list gives suggestions for additions to the stuffing.

Stuffings:

*Chopped chives or parsley or other herbs with garlic and yoghurt.
*Chopped cooked mushrooms.
*Chopped or minced cooked meat, game, poultry or ham.
*Grated cheese and ham.
*Scrambled egg and parsley.
*Chopped cooked chicken livers.
*Onion, grated raw, or chopped and cooked.
*Flaked cooked fish or fried and chopped roes.
*Fried chopped kidneys.
*Chopped fried bacon.
*Cooked cabbage or spinach.
*Cooked sausage meat and onion.
*Aioli, a garlic mayonnaise.

Pomme Gratin Dauphinois

Peel the potatoes and slice them very thin. Wash the slices in cold water to remove some of the starch. Dry thoroughly and arrange a layer in a well buttered shallow baking dish. Sprinkle on a chopped clove of garlic for each pound of potatoes, salt and pepper then continue the layers and seasoning until all the potatoes are used. Pour on ½ pint of single cream for each pound of potatoes, then fleck the surface with butter and a little freshly grated nutmeg. Cook in a hot pre-heated oven (1½ hours).

Sautéed Potatoes

Peel some boiled potatoes and slice them about ¼ inch thick. Heat a little butter or oil in a frying pan and keep the potatoes moving, turning them until they are well browned and have absorbed the fat. Serve hot with salt, pepper and a good sprinkling of chopped parsley.

Pommes de Terre Lyonnaise

Add freshly fried sliced onions to sautéed potatoes and serve immediately. The onions take about 10 minutes and the potatoes about 15 minutes to fry to a golden brown. For each pound of potatoes use a medium onion and 2 oz of butter.

Gnocchi

2 lb red floury potatoes, 2 eggs, 1 oz butter, 2 tablespoons grated parmesan, and some flour.

Bake the potatoes then split them and take out the pulp. Mix this with the butter and half the cheese. Beat the eggs and mash them into the mixture; finally add flour until you have a thick modelling paste. Flour your hands and make the paste into little sausages. Put these in boiling salted water: when they rise to the surface they are ready. Remove, serve covered with hot tomato or béchamel sauce, sprinkling the remaining cheese on top.

Potatoes in the French Kitchen

The French have a good variety of distinct ways of cooking potatoes. This list defines some of the more important methods.

Alumettes - cut like matchsticks, fried.
Alsacienne - new potatoes tossed with butter, bits of bacon, small onions and herbs.
Anglaise - boiled.
Anna - neatly arranged thin round slices baked in butter.
Berny - balls of minced truffles and mashed potatoes, fried.
Boulangère - sliced onions, fried, with sliced potatoes cooked in the oven with meat stock.
Bretonne - cubes of potatoes with garlic, onion and tomatoes cooked in stock.
Cepaux - shavings, deep fried.
Chambèry - slices of boiled potatoes in layers with butter and cheese, browned in the oven.
Chips - fried.
Crème - boiled, sliced and then stewed in milk served with cream.
Dauphine - mashed with butter and egg yolk, mixed with puff pastry, deep fried, as small
    cylinders, egg and breadcrumbed.
Duchesse - mashed with butter and egg yolk, piped, brushed with egg, browned in oven.
Au Four - baked in their jackets.
Au Gratin - mashed with butter, egg yolk, cream, grated cheese, covered with breadcrumbs,
    browned in the oven.
Maître d'hôtel - same as crème potatoes sprinkled with parsley.
Noisettes - cut like marbles, cooked in butter, served with herbs.
Paille - cut like straws, deep fried.
Parmentier - used on French menus to mean potatoes.
Persillées - new potatoes, cooked in stock, served with butter and parsley.
Provençale - sautéed with minced garlic.
Savoyarde - like Dauphinoise using stock instead of milk.
Voisin - are Pommes Anna with some grated cheese and a pinch of nutmeg in each layer.

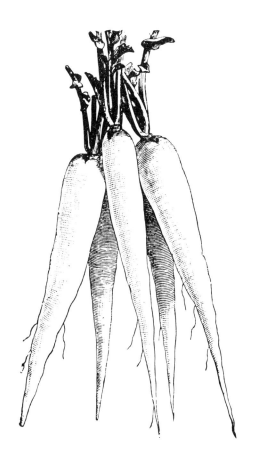

RADISHES

This, pungent, fleshy, snappy and peppery root can be small or large and round or long and tapering in shape. It can be pink, white, scarlet or brown, purple, grey or yellow depending on the variety and when harvested. Radishes can be cooked like salsify, but they are not meant to be and are much better eaten raw.

Mouli

Long white radish-tasting root that is sometimes known as Japanese horseradish. In Japan it is grated very fine and used as a condiment.

SALSIFY

Also called salsafy and sometimes vegetable oyster because the long white roots boiled and tender do have a very faint sea flavour. Scrape and parboil in salted water with a drop of vinegar or lemon juice in it to stop the roots discolouring, then finish cooking in hot butter.

The young leaves can be braised or put into spring salads.

Salsify Fritters

Parboil salsify, drain and cut into 3-inch lengths. Dip in batter and fry in deep fat or oil until crisp and golden. Drain and serve hot with chopped or whole fried parsley.

Salsify with Cheese

Boil until just tender and cut into 3-inch lengths. Put these in a baking dish, pour over white sauce and cover the top with lots of grated cheese and breadcrumbs and dots of butter. Brown in a hot oven or under the grill.

SCORZONERA

Long black roots and very like salsify, though perhaps a little better. French cookery books hardly distinguish between the two. It is simple to cook and all the recipes for salsify are recommended for scorzonera. The leaves make an excellent green salad.

SEA KALE

This grew wild on most of the coasts of Western Europe. The white stalks, with the spinach-like leaves removed, can be used uncooked for salads. It is good boiled, braised or baked in white sauce. Never overcook it or else it toughens and the good nutty taste is lost.

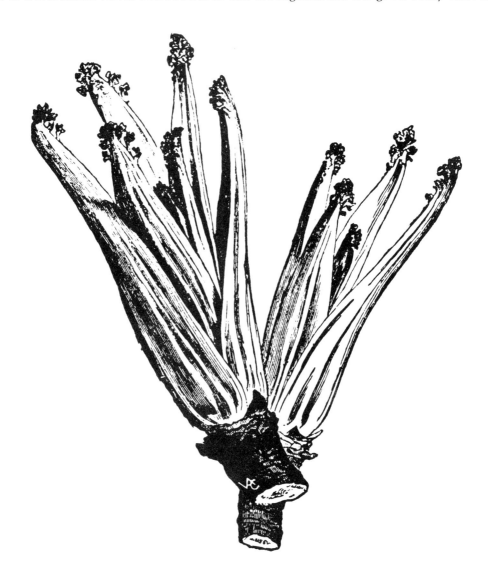

SPINACH

"I know not wherefore it is good savinge to fill the belly."

Turner's *Herbal*, 1568

"Tis laxative and emollient and therefore profitable for the aged."

John Evelyn, *Acetaria*, 1699

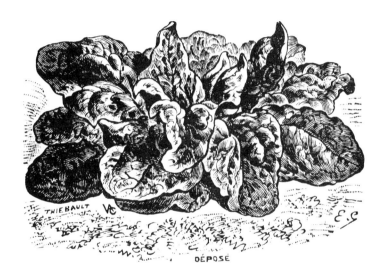

Spinach shrinks in the cooking so allow at least ½ lb per person.

To prepare, first sort through and throw away any weeds or wilted pieces. Wash in three or four changes of cold water and then pack it into a saucepan that may look ridiculously large after the spinach has cooked. Add only a dessertspoonful of water and cook it slowly. Stir at first to make sure that the bottom leaves do not stick to the saucepan, then stir in some salt. Usually 10 minutes' cooking is enough to make every leaf tender. Draining it thoroughly is difficult; push it down firmly into a colander using a plate to press it. Slice the leaves into smaller pieces while it is still in the colander, put back the plate and press out the last drops of liquid. Buttered spinach is prepared by stirring butter into the cooked spinach.

Spinach with Cream

Cook the spinach and stir into it 2 tablespoons of bubbling hot double cream, a scrape of nutmeg and some pepper. Serve really hot. Good with liver, ham, steak, chops or with a fried or poached egg.

A useful and grander elaboration is to add a tablespoon of sherry with the cream and to serve sprinkled with cubes of fried bread.

Spinach with Cheese

On fried bread this makes an hors d'oeuvre or it can be eaten with fish or egg.

One pound of cooked spinach is mixed with 2 oz of grated cheese, baked in a moderate oven for ½ an hour to heat it up. To brown the top, cover with another ounce of grated cheese and a tablespoon of breadcrumbs and put under the grill.

Spinach Quiche

Use the same proportions as though making leek quiche. Mix ½ lb of cooked spinach with 2 tablespoons of chopped onion that has been cooked for two minutes in an ounce of butter. Season with salt and pepper, and a scrape or two of nutmeg. Stir together with the mixture of eggs and cream and pour into an eight-inch pastry shell. Sprinkle with cheese, dot with butter and bake until just set in a moderate oven (25 minutes). Brown off the top by putting under the grill.

This is served hot or cold, but I like it better cold.

Spinach with Poached Eggs *(Yorkshire manuscript dated 1769)*

"Take two or three handfuls of young spinach, pick it from the stalks, wash and drain it very clean, put it in a pan with a lump of butter and a little salt, and keep stirring it all the time till it be done enough then take it out and squeeze out the water. Chop it and add a little more butter, lay it in your dish in quarters, and betwixt every quarter a poached egg and one in the middle.

Fry some snippets of white bread and put them into your spinach and so serve it up."

SWEDE

Swede is an abbreviation of Swedish turnip. In America it is a rutabaga, it has also been called a Russian turnip and turnip-rooted cabbage. Its introduction to England in the 17th century was revolutionary for the cattle farmers. In most of Europe its delicious orange flesh is still only fed to cattle.

Swedes are good peeled, cut into cubes and boiled until tender, or just mashed. They are an asset to vegetable pies, soups and stews and sliced thin and lightly braised in the Chinese manner, can be tasted at their best. Swedes may also be cooked in any way suitable for turnips.

SWEETCORN

Corn on the cob may be put in boiling salted water and simmered for up to 20 minutes. The leaves may be removed before cooking. Serve with wooden prongs or forks in each end and provide melted butter, salt and pepper. Very fresh corn cooks in half the time which is why the much shorter time is sometimes quoted, particularly by Americans.

Young fresh corn is delicious cooked by toasting under a grill and then serving in the same way already described. Baby corns are best cooked like this or in the Chinese manner of high speed braising, either on their own or with other vegetables.

Succotash

Sweetcorn boiled and taken off the cob is mixed with an equal amount of Lima, haricot or broadbeans already soaked and boiled tender. Season mixture to taste and just stir in a little cream or white sauce.

SWEET POTATO

Like the ordinary potato, the sweet potato is of American origin and is cultivated for its tubers. It grows in the tropics where it is commonly boiled and mashed and served as a sweet. In Africa it is used to give a sweet, scented element in some spiced peppery stews. In the Pacific it is often baked with orange juice, brown sugar and butter.

Yams

Yams are rhizomes of Chinese origin. Some varieties grow to giant size. The common yam is also known as the Indian potato and is often thought to be the same as the sweet potato. It is cooked in all the many ways suitable for potatoes.

TOMATOES

A fruit grown in England mainly as a garden ornament and known as love-apples until the first World War, the tomato now seems to be regarded as a necessity of life judging by the high prices people are prepared to pay for them.

English tomatoes are grown in heated glass houses for the earlier crop. Starting in May with the season extending to October, many tomatoes come from the Lea Valley, from Sussex near Worthing, from Lancashire near Blackpool — the nearest England comes to suntraps.

From outside England Jersey and Guernsey tomatoes are well advertised and provide one in every six tomatoes sold. A lot come from Holland during the same season. The Canary and Spanish tomatoes do not compete during the English growing season.

To peel a tomato, skewer with a fork and heat the skin very rapidly in a gas flame or in briskly boiling water.

Baked Tomatoes

Wash and dry the tomatoes and take out any stalks. Put them, stem hole down, on a lightly oiled baking tray. Brush them with oil and sprinkle salt and pepper over them. Bake them in the middle of a preheated medium oven for about 10 minutes. They are cooked when their skins break a little but if they are left too long they burst.

Tomatoes cooked in this way look very decorative, especially if parsley, fresh chopped chives, or basil is sprinkled on them before serving.

Stuffed Tomatoes

Choose large, ripe but still firm tomatoes, cut them in half crosswise and gently scoop out the centres. Sprinkle the halves with a little salt and pepper.

For 4 tomatoes:

1 clove of garlic, mashed, 2 tablespoons chopped shallot or onion, ½ teaspoon chopped basil, 1 teaspoon chopped parsley, a pinch of thyme, 1 oz breadcrumbs (you can substitute cheese for a more nutritious dish), and 1½ tablespoons of olive oil.

Mix all the ingredients together and season to taste. Fill each half tomato with some of the mixture. Bake in a preheated medium oven until the tomatoes are tender but still shapely (15 minutes).

Also try the stuffing suggested for aubergines. Stuffed tomatoes make a good hors d'oeuvre or a light meal. They also go well with most fairly dry meat, fish, poultry and egg dishes.

Scalloped Tomatoes *(18th-century Sussex recipe)*

"Put alternate layers of tomatoes and breadcrumbs in a pie dish. Let the top layer be of tomatoes. Sprinkle bits of butter over. Season well and bake."
Note: butter the pie dish and season and dot each layer with butter.

TURNIPS

"Turnepes being well boyled in water, and after with fatte fleshe, norysheth moche."
Elyot, 1539.

Glazed Turnips

Choose turnips as small as possible and all about the same size; if only large ones are available, cut them into quarters and peel them. Scrub them clean and scrub off any unpleasant spots. Heat enough butter to cover the bottom of a flameproof dish and put the turnips onto this; dot a little butter on them and spoon over them 5 or 6 tablespoons of stock or water. Sprinkle them with sugar, salt and pepper. Cook gently over a low heat for 45 minutes. Turn the turnips over once or twice; they will glisten in a pale brown sauce.

Add a squeeze of lemon juice and some parsley before serving.

Turnip Casserole with Ham

2 lbs turnips, 1 dessertspoon flour, ¼ lb ham or bacon, ½ pint stock or bouillon, 1 teaspoon sage, 1 medium onion, ½ oz butter, sugar.

Trim and peel the turnips and if they are large, two inches or more, cut them into quarters. Cut the onion, ham or bacon and brown them in the butter (5 minutes). Stir in a dessertspoon of flour, and cook slowly for 2 minutes. Away from the heat, blend in the stock, with the sage, some sugar and seasonings to taste. Simmer for a minute and then add the turnips; cover the pan and simmer until the turnips are tender (30 minutes).

Mashed Turnips

Prepare and cook the turnips. Add butter, milk or cream, liquidize or push through a sieve; season and serve hot. Well cooked potatoes can be mashed with the turnips. Turnips cooked like this are usually eaten with fish or white meat.

Turnip Relish *(Chinese)*

Take 8 oz of clean, sliced turnips and sprinkle with 1 tablespoon of salt. Leave them to stand for several hours, preferably overnight. Do not worry if they discolour as this will be rectified during the cooking. Fry briskly in 1 tablespoon of oil for 5 minutes, then add 1 tablespoon of vinegar, stir and remove from the heat. Pour over some sesame oil and serve hot or cold.

Turnip Tops

Wash 1 lb of turnip tops and put in a colander. Pour boiling water over to soften them. Shred and quick fry for 3 minutes. Add salt and serve. (Note: bad smell, good taste!)

Turnip Stalks

"Take their stalks (when they begin to run up to seed) as far as they will easily break downwards: peel and tie them in Bundles. These boiling them as they do Sparagus are to be eaten with melted Butter."

Elyot, dated 1539.

HOGARTH AND COVENT GARDEN

The painter Sir James Thornhill, decorator of the Painted Hall at Greenwich and the inner dome of St Paul's Cathedral, lived until his death in 1734 at No. 12, The Piazza, at the other corner of the square, in the most easterly house in the North range and today the West end of the Floral Hall. Hogarth, Thornhill's son-in-law, also lived at No.12 and it was from there that together they ran their painting Academy.

Hogarth's print is an early view of the Piazza's descent into rowdy iniquity. By 1776 the fall had proceeded so far that Covent Garden is become "the great square of Venus, and its purlieus are crowded with the votaries of this Goddess. The jelly-houses are now become the resort of abandoned rakes and shameless prostitutes. These and the taverns afford an ample supply of provisions for the flesh; while others abound for the consummation of the desires which are thus excited. For this vile end the bagnios and lodging-houses are near at hand".

Tom King's coffee-house had a considerable reputation as the mixing bowl for the noblemen, rakes and market ruffians. Tom King, from a well-to-do Yorkshire family, had run away from Eton in 1713. His widow, Moll King, continued to run the shop with a scandalous lack of propriety. In 1739 Moll was fined £200 and imprisoned for three months — the maximum penalty for keeping a disorderly house. Since Hogarth's day the coffee stall has moved under the church portico and is likely to continue on the same site, providing welcome refreshments.

Right: Hogarth's self-portrait

Left: Hogarth's "Morning", 1720

VEGETABLES COOKED TOGETHER

Santana Mexico

Rules, with its rich Edwardian décor, is the most famous restaurant in Covent Garden. The food is mainly traditional and English: steak and kidney pies, jugged hare, roast beef with Yorkshire pudding and game in season. Founded in 1798 as an oyster bar, it now has every wall covered with pictures that tell its history — portraits of Dickens, Thackeray, Edward VII and of his friend Lily Langtrey, prints by Hogarth, theatre bills and much more.

Mr André Chion, the head chef, makes a mixture of vegetables for garnishing roast loin of veal, and he gave this recipe:

"Diced courgettes, aubergines, red, yellow and green peppers, chopped shallots, garlic, tomatoes and a spoonful of tomato purée. Season with salt, pepper and a little sugar.

Stir all the vegetables together and set them cooking with just a tiny drop of water. Once this has boiled, turn the heat right down and leave them, covered, to cook for about 24 minutes or until they are all tender."

TWO JAPANESE RECIPES

The following two Japanese recipes were given me by Mr Susumu Okada of the Ajimua Japanese Restaurant in Endell Street. The nice delicacy of treatment was apparent from his precise and patient description. No other cook I have talked to prescribed the capacity of a cup or specified the temperature of the frying oil. These recipes are the measure of experience.

Vegetable Tempura

The ingredients: green peppers, seaweed, spring onions, parsley, onions (diced and fixed on toothpicks), broccoli, cauliflower, asparagus — "and even bananas". Cut the spring onions to 2-3 inches and all the other vegetables to mouth-sized pieces.

The batter: beat together two eggs and two cupfuls of water (400 cc's). Mix in white flour until you have the consistency of double cream, but do not beat or whisk the flour as this releases glutens and makes the mixture too sticky to fry "dry". A few lumps will not matter. Ice cubes can be used to keep the batter cool.

The sauce: 2 cupfuls of clear fish stock, ½ cup of soya sauce, ½ cup of sweet wine, preferably Japanese Minn or Chinese Sake with some sugar added, but medium sherry will do. Bring these to the boil and then add one tablespoon of finely grated white radish (mouli) for each person.

Heat some oil, the finest possible vegetable, sesame or sunflower oil, but not olive oil, to 160-180°C just before it smokes. Put the vegetables into the batter so that just half is coated. Fry each one for just 20 seconds. As all the vegetables can be eaten raw they only need to heat up and the batter will cook very quickly. Put them in the sauce before serving.

Yasai — Itame

Cut fresh vegetables into tiny thin sticks. Use mushrooms, green peppers, spring onions, onions, carrots, potatoes and shredded root ginger. Cut them all to the same size. Heat ½ cup of oil in a frying pan and put the hardest vegetables in first. Ginger, carrot, onion, spring onion, potatoes in that order every 10 seconds. As soon as they take the heat from the oil you are ready to put in the other vegetables. Add some salt, white pepper, a sprinkle of soya sauce, some saki or dry sherry and when it is hot it is ready. Do not cook it, just heat it and eat it.

Saucisses Aux Choux *(from Marcel Boulestin)*

"Put a piece of bacon, about half a pound in weight, in a large saucepan with water, broken pepper, salt and the classical bay leaf, thyme and parsley tied together; cook it for about one hour and a half. Then remove it, if you are a careful person and want to use it at its best for something else (or cold in the Irish peasant fashion) — or recklessly leave it in if you do not mind. Anyhow, the water is sufficiently flavoured by now for our purpose. Bring it once more to the boil and then throw in your cabbage, previously well washed and cut in smallish pieces.

While the cabbage is cooking grill the sausages (the long French ones made of pork are the only possible ones for this dish) and keep them warm. Drain the cabbage well, add more salt and pepper, a little grated nutmeg, a small piece of butter, and put half of it in a fireproof dish, then with the sausages on this bed, add the rest of the cabbage. Pour a cupful of good beef stock over it. Cook in a moderate oven with the lid on for about half an hour or so. This dish if properly prepared, is quite delicious."

Ragoût de Boeuf *(from Marcel Boulestin)*

"The preliminary frying of the vegetables for this dish makes all the difference to it and gives it a flavour quite apart from that of an ordinary stew.

Clean and peel the following vegetables and then cut them into slices: 3 medium sized carrots, 3 onions, and several tomatoes. Place them in an earthenware stew-pan and fry them in olive oil — or butter, if you prefer it — until almost cooked. Meanwhile you should have browned your beef for a few minutes in butter. Add the meat to the vegetables, and then one tumblerful of cold water, salt and pepper. Let the ragoût simmer gently for at least one hour, keeping the lid on the pan.''

Thiou Diene *(Senegalese)*

This fish and vegetable recipe was given to me by Paolo Diop, the Senegalese chef of the Calabash restaurant in the Africa Centre in King Street. He has cooked in France, Italy, and, of course, Africa where some distinctive regional cooking is found, but he claims, it is unjustly neglected in Europe.

For 10 people:
2 lbs fish (dorado*), 3 sweet potatoes, ½ lb cabbage, a piece of pumpkin, 1 lb potatoes, 5 carrots, 5 turnips, ½ lb tomato purée, ½ lb onions, 1 clove garlic, a large cupful of groundnut oil, a bay leaf and some chili.

Chop the potatoes and sauté them in the oil, remove and set aside. Put in the fish, sliced, and seal it over a good heat, remove and set aside. Fry the onion and garlic until golden brown, add the tomato purée thinned with a little water and put the fish slices back with the bay leaf, salt and pepper. Leave simmering for one minute then add a pint and a half of boiling water. Put all the vegetables in; those taking the longest to cook put in first. Remove the fish after 20 minutes and set aside to keep warm, continue cooking until the vegetables are tender and the sauce well thickened, then return the fish and serve hot on rice.

*The dorado (sometimes called the dolphin fish), is a good-looking green coloured fish found in the Indian Ocean. It is a muscle-meat fish and perhaps the best alternative would be a mackerel. The Romans ate dorado, bringing it to the table live in a tank and then killing it, because as it dies it changes from green to brilliant turquoise and finally to a pure gold colour.

Normandy Pie

Cut up potatoes, carrots, celery and any other vegetable except cabbage into a pie-dish. Add a handful of well soaked peas, two hard-boiled eggs, a little chopped onion and parsley, and a bit of butter, pepper and salt. Moisten with stock or cream. Cover with a very light crust and bake.

Chinese Mixed Vegetables

2 oz each of onion, cabbage, and mushroom. Dice. Cut 2 oz of broccoli and French beans into one-inch lengths.

Put the French beans and cabbage into fast boiling water for 3 minutes, drain and rinse under a cold tap. Heat the oil. Quick fry the onion, cabbage and French beans, then add the mushrooms and broccoli. Fry for two minutes more, season with salt and serve.

Fried Mixed Vegetables *(winter vegetables)*

4 oz turnips, 4 oz carrots, 4 oz celery, 4 leeks, 1 teaspoon vinegar, 1 teaspoon salt, 1 tablespoon oil, 1 teaspoon sesame oil.

Slice all the vegetables as thinly as possible and in fine strips. Heat the oil and fry all the vegetables together quickly for 5 minutes. Add salt and vinegar and continue frying for 3 minutes. Eat it hot, or allow to cool and add sesame oil.

Vegetable Pie *(a manuscript recipe from Kent dated 1850)*

"Required, one onion, one carrot, one turnip, one stick of celery, one handful of green peas (if in season), half an ounce of sago, one ounce of butter, pepper and salt, pie crust. Cut all the vegetables small, and stew them with the sago and butter in a very little water until nearly cooked. Then put in a pie dish, cover with crust, and bake about half an hour. Any other vegetables may be used at pleasure. Mushrooms are always an improvement."

Hodge Podge of Mutton *(Kent, 1809)*

"Cut a neck or loin of mutton into steaks (i.e. chops or cutlets). Take off all the fat, then put the steaks into a pitcher or jar, with lettuce, turnips, carrots, two cucumbers cut in quarters, four or five onions, and pepper and salt; you must not put any water to it; stop the pitcher very close, then set it in a pan of boiling water; let it boil four hours. Keep the pan supplied with fresh boiling water as it wastes."

[Today this could be cooked in the oven if your oven thermostat can give you about 212°F. In this manner you could dispense with the troublesome pan of boiling water.]

Bouquetier

The Neal Street Restaurant highly prizes a smart turnout and a good appearance. Mr Gonzales, the chef, knows that every customer has his own taste in food; he reckons there are individual tastes in colours as well.

"Make your own selection of vegetables, for example carrots, spinach, yellow pepper, mushrooms. Cook each individually in butter. It is then not too difficult to have all ready at the same time. Arrange them in lines of colour on a large dish."

Stovies *(from The Shetland Cookery Book by Margaret B. Stout)*

1½ lbs mutton, 1 lb potatoes, pepper and salt, 1 onion, ½ small turnip and 1 tablespoon suet.

"Cut the mutton up finely; chop the suet; put these into the pan and pour on enough boiling water to cover; simmer gently for 1 hour. Chop the onion finely, cut potatoes and turnip up coarsely; add these to stew and cook gently for another hour; season and serve hot."

Vegetable Stew

This is a simple example of a plain vegetable stew; make it in a heavy casserole or saucepan.

Chopped parsley, a clove of garlic, a tomato, celery, an onion, a shallot, carrots, a potato, a turnip, butter or oil, salt and pepper

Heat the oil or butter and gently fry the garlic, onion and shallot; let them brown lightly before adding the other vegetables prepared and cut quite small. Turn the stew in the oil, warm it through until it starts to sweat. Season, then moisten with water; cover, and allow it to simmer until tender (30 minutes). The pieces of potato will disintegrate and thicken the stew but if you want them to remain whole put them in 20 minutes after the other vegetables.

Serve plain or with grated cheese. If you wish to thicken the stew more, remove the saucepan from the heat, allow to cool for a few minutes and then using a wooden spoon briskly stir in an egg.

Vegetable Hot Pot *(a manuscript recipe from Kent, dated 1850)*

"Take two large potatoes, one stick of celery, one large carrot, one large onion, butter, pepper and salt. Slice the vegetables, put them in layers in a pie-dish, with a layer of potatoes at the top. Pour in a quarter of a pint of boiling water. Set the dish in a cool oven and let it simmer for one and a half hours. Lay little pieces of butter on the top, and serve very hot. This method of cooking the vegetables preserves the flavour far better than boiling would do."

Ratatouille

The usual vegetables for this Provençal stew are aubergines, courgettes, tomatoes, onions and peppers. The amount of each can be varied according to taste, availability and price. Garlic can be a major flavour or not feature at all. The vegetables must, however, be stewed in olive oil or in a cheaper but good oil with enough olive oil to give flavour to the whole.

2 onions, 2 aubergines, 2 large red peppers, 6 courgettes, 6 tomatoes, 1 clove of garlic and basil, fresh or dried.

Cut the onions into thin slices or cubes, not less than ¼ inch thick or they will not stay in whole pieces when they are cooked. Cut the peppers in half and, discarding the seeds, cut into strips. Skin the tomatoes (hold them on a fork over a flame or in boiling water). Coarsely chop the aubergines and courgettes.
    Heat the oil in a pan and put in the onions.
    When they are soft add the aubergines, courgettes, peppers and garlic. Cover and cook gently for half an hour, then add the tomatoes and basil, salt and pepper to taste. Cook until all the vegetables are soft but not mushy (½ hour).
    Ratatouille is good hot or cold, as a vegetable accompanying plain roast or grilled meat, or on its own to begin a meal.

Left: Pope, 1737   *Above: the Piazza, 1764*

POPE AND THE COFFEE HOUSES

When a young lad, Pope pestered his friends to take him to Wills's Coffee House, at the corner of Russell Street and Bow Street, to gaze upon Dryden (1631-1700). Afterwards he described him as "plump, with a fresh colour, with a down look, and not very conversable".

A list of some of the Coffee Houses includes Buttons, the Rose next to Drury Lane Theatre, Tom's at 17 Russell Street, The Bedford and Sam's. Among the people who were found there were Dr Johnson, Smollett, Fielding, Lord Clive, Garrick, Oliver Goldsmith, the Marquis of Granby, Addison, the Duke of Northumberland, Swift and Steele.

The Coffee Houses were great meeting places for every sort of man. The establishment of the Theatre Royal (1663) and the Covent Garden Theatre (1732) encouraged people to move back to live in the area and these people in their turn gave the Coffee Houses their great lease of life. All this time the Market became more and more active but at the price of many disputes between the tenants and the Duke of Bedford regarding the terms of leases and the stall-holders' obligations to their landlord, especially in regard to tolls charged on produce brought to the Market.

"A MASSIVE LOAD OF FLESH"

From a contemporary newspaper report comes the story of an Irish basket woman who for a wager carried "the uncommonly big gentleman" in her basket from the Market to the Elephant and Castle within the given time of 25 minutes. At Waterloo Bridge she was given a glass of gin and a shilling but at the Coburg Theatre the unwieldy gentleman thrust his legs out, thus influencing the betting against her. Threatening to throw him in the ditch in order to keep him still she won the wager and was greeted on arrival by a large crowd.

*A WALK FROM THE ALDWYCH TO COVENT GARDEN UNDERGROUND
STATION, SUMMER 1974*

The fourth hysterical year at the Strand Theatre, No Sex Please, We're British, *"the
audience rolled about", and on the left, established 30 years, Curly's Fruit Barrow, rain
or shine, on the corner of Catherine Street and the Aldwych. Pass a rising tide of office
workers. This is the eastern end of theatreland, and, up the Aldwych, the Aldwych
displays such good taste that the billboards can't be read. To the left is* Oh Calcutta!
*at the Duchess; ahead, the Theatre Royal, reached by passing Polland, the Fruiterers' and
Florists' sundriesman, with emerald astroturf, bridal bouquet holders in cardboard boxes,
plastic Wedgwood.*

*Across Tavistock Street, K.M. Ltd, the cut-price bargainers, hold the other corner
spellbound with fancy goods, novelties. Then restaurants, cafés, pubs: the Opera Tavern,
Nell of Old Drury. A shrine across the road, for Augustus Harris, erected by public
subscription, his noble head supported by one leering cherub and another scowling. In
Russell Street were coffee houses for Dyrden, Pepys, Dr Johnson, Fielding, but no plaques
there, or memories. Another theatre, the Fortune, and further east, a rotund concrete and
glass thing by Siefert.*

*On towards the Piazza, see the bow in Bow Street, Royal Opera House left, earliest
police station right, example of Wrenaissance. Left and right through No. 4 gate into the
flower market; J.H. Pardoe Ltd reeking of geranium, Thos Leonard empty, gone; has he
moved already? In their scented, vaulted hall with its liquid, lambent light, are they
happy to be moving? No. Bloom, bud, flower, blossom, shrub, plant; all colours, every
shape. Exit towards No. 2, turn right and stand, back to Barney Springer, Merchant, at
the corner of Russell Street. The central building, the Dedicated Market, topped with
cherubs and windswept maidens hauling garlands up the flagpole. Notice of ownership:
Duke of Bedford 1830.*

*Round the Piazza anticlockwise. The Tin Market, a shed active with nameplates, stands
corner to corner against the Floral Hall, where there are no flowers, but foreign fruits.
Joe's caravan is shut for teas and snacks; is it too soon or too late? the corner of James
Street gives the view, to the west, of Lord Archer's studded door at the end of Bedford
Chambers' busy colonnade and, looking to the south, read there the Russell family's coat
of arms:* Che Sara, Sara *over the Market's central axis.*

*Going up sunlit James Street, porters basking on trolleys. On the left are seven separate
fruit and vegetable traders, including Don Wuillie's curvaceous fascia board. Old Red
Lion faces Nag's Head. On the right, ten separate traders. Turn left at the top, and the
underground station, tiled and Art Nouveau; scent of fruit and veg almost until the train
arrives at the next station.*

HERBS

"Anything green that grew out of the mould
Was an excellent herb to our fathers of old."
— Rudyard Kipling

ANGELICA

It is said that during the Plague an angel appeared with a root of angelica in his mouth; this was commended to drive away the "pestilentiall aire".

Every part of this plant has some use: oil from the roots and seeds flavours liqueurs and wines, the leaves flavour cooked fruits and make teas, the stalks and leaf stems are candied and used as cake and dessert decoration.

BALM

Also known as lemon balm, its leaves are used in potpourris, teas, wine and fruit cups, and old recipe healing ointments. A few dried balm leaves in a pot of ordinary tea make the drink more refreshing.

BASIL

Originally from India but usually now from the Mediterranean area. Its strong, mouth-watering smell and taste stay when it is dried. Basil has a particular affinity to tomato either cooked or raw. A very good addition to vinaigrette or chopped finely and added to tomato soup or salad. It also goes well with cheese, eggs, fish and green salads.

BAY LEAVES

From the shores of the Mediterranean, the leaves were the wreaths that crowned the heroes of ancient Greece and Rome. In French and old English cookery books it is known as laurel from its Latin name *Laurus nobilis.* Bay trees are handsome and it may be that more are sold through Covent Garden as decoration than are branches of fresh bay to greengrocers for their customers. A bay leaf is used to flavour any number of things: soups, stews, meats, poultry, fish and even milk puddings.

"neither witch nor devil, thunder nor lightening will hurt a man where a bay tree is"
                                                                                Culpepper.

William Turner, a barber, lived and worked on the site of what is now 21 Maiden Lane. Below the house was a tavern known as the Cider Cellar. His son, J.M.W. Turner, born there in 1775, became the great English painter of light and colour. He returned to 26 Maiden Lane to live in an apartment "small and ill calculated for a painter" from 1790 until the end of the century. The following recipe is as it appears in Turner's sketch book dated 1798:

"Recipe for making an Efficable ointment for Cuts.

Solomans Seal — leaves and buds, Comfrey — do. Bay, Elder, Valerian

An equal quantity to which may be added a handfull of parsley these herbs must be cut small bruised in a stone mortor boil for some hours in a Bell bowled Kettle over a slow fire in a sufficient quantity of unwashed butter to make the Herbs thoroughly moist it must stand 10 to 12 days after which strain thro a Cloth, the Juice then to be boiled and well skimm'd and run into small Jars or Pots.

Given by Miss Narraway of Bristol."

BERGAMOT

The scented leaves of this herb are recommended as an accompaniment to pork or, finely chopped, added to salad. The red pom-pom flowers are also a good and pretty addition to a salad.

BORAGE

Borage was once a very highly thought of and much used herb. The flowers made a tea which made the drinker happy. The leaves, as well as being mixed in salads, were used to cleanse and strengthen skin and body.

"Take 2 lb barley or bean meal, 8 lb bran, and a few handfuls of borage leaves. Boil these ingredients in a sufficient quantity of spring water. Nothing cleanes and softens the skin like this bath." (A cosmetic bath from "The Toilet of Flora" in *The Scented Garden*, by E. S. Rohde).

CHERVIL

"The garden chervil doth at first somewhat resemble parsley, but after it is better grown the leaves are cut in and jagged, resembling hemlock, being a little hairy, and of a whitish green colour, sometimes turning reddish in the summer, with the stalks also; it riseth a little above half a foot high, bearing white flowers in spiked tufts, which turn into long and round seeds pointed at the ends, and blackish when they are ripe."

The leaves have a spicy, slightly aniseed taste. It is good with eggs, in soups, salads, quiches and green and bean vegetable dishes.

CHIVES

With thin, green grass-like leaves chives resemble and are related to onions, leeks, shallots and garlic. Chives add flavour to soft cheeses, salads, egg dishes and fish.

GARLIC

Grow to love garlic and you are tempted to use it lavishly, raw or cooked. But, whatever your feelings, it is good for the digestion and for the complexion. For salads, finely chop and add to the vinaigrette, rub onto a piece of bread and leave at the bottom of the bowl or simply rub the bowl with it. In meat or vegetable stews which can take some time to cook, several cloves or segments of the bulb give a delicious taste without being overwhelming. Crush a clove or two of garlic into mashed potatoes. With a knife poke small pieces into lamb or mutton before roasting.

Garlic Bread

Finely chop or pound 3 cloves of garlic and mash this into ¼ lb of softened butter. Slice a loaf of bread but not quite through, leaving enough to hold the loaf together. Generously cover the slices with the garlic mixture. Push the loaf together again and bake it in a hot oven until warm all through (15 minutes).

Aioli

Aioli is a rich garlic mayonnaise from the South of France. Crush and pound as much garlic as you like and add this to the mayonnaise as you make it.

Spaghetti al Pesto

Pesto is a garlic and basil sauce from Genoa. Katherine Hamnett, who designs and produces beautiful clothes at the premises of her firm Tutabankem in Shelton Street, gave me a favourite recipe.

"This is really easy to make and everybody seems to like it — the most important thing to remember is to use the best ingredients. So for 4 people you need 1 lb of the fresh home-made spaghetti from Camisa, at the end of Old Compton Street about 6 oz of unsalted butter, and 2 tablespoonsful of Olio Sasso olive oil, 2 large cloves of garlic, a large pinch of salt and about a dozen fresh basil leaves.

Boil a medium-sized pan of salted water and when it is boiling put the spaghetti in. Stir it once or twice so it does not all stick together and let it boil for 5 minutes.

Crush the garlic and the basil and mix with the salt and butter.

Drain the spaghetti when cooked and then mix in the garlic, basil, salt and butter and olive oil. Stir it over the heat for 30 seconds, sprinkle with freshly grated Parmesan and serve."

MARJORAM

This is a herb that seems to improve with drying. It is recommended with meat in stews and pies, with eggs, fish, and mixed with cream cheese. Wild marjoram is oregano.

MINT

"Mints put into milk, it neyther sufferth the same to curde, nor to be come thick, insomuch that layed in curded milke, this would bring the same thinne againe."
The Good Housewife's Handmaid, 1588.

Mint is a most popular herb in England; strangely enough many Continentals shudder with horror at its use. Be that as it may it still flavours our lamb, potatoes, peas, fruitcups and toothpaste.

Mint Sauce

Curly mint is often used.

Put a dessertspoon of chopped mint into a jug with some sugar, hot water, and vinegar. For a change, try sweetening with honey and using lemon juice instead of vinegar.

Sandwiches

Tasty brown bread sandwiches are created with chopped mint on honey, or chopped mint on cheese.

Mint Julep

The eau-de-cologne mint is best. Crush a large bunch of mint and add to it 1 cup of pineapple juice, the juice of 4 lemons and some sugar. Leave the mixture to stand for several hours, stirring occasionally, then strain it into a jug together with ice-cubes, slices of lemon, sprigs of mint and 3 bottles of dry ginger ale.

Mint Jelly

1¼ pints wine vinegar, 12 oz sugar, ½ pint hot water, 1½ oz gelatine or pectin, 4 tablespoons chopped mint and some salt.

Boil the water, vinegar, sugar, mint, with a pinch of salt. Allow the mixture to cool a little and then dissolve the gelatine in it. Stir occasionally before putting it to set in small pots. Store in a cool place.

Mint Relish

A handful of mint well pounded with some salt, pepper and the juice of a lemon. This is good served with curry.

PARSLEY

Eaten fresh it has health advantages including vitamin C, carotene, and minerals. It makes good salad on its own and can be added to almost everything savoury. The Mediterranean varieties are more fern-like in their appearance.

Fried Parsley

Often rather sandy; if you need to wash it see that it is dry before frying. Deep fry for one minute when it should still be quite green but crisp.

Parsley Butter

For baked potatoes and grilled meat or fish, a dessertspoonful of finely chopped parsley, together with a few drops of lemon juice are mashed in up to 4 oz of butter. This, when chilled, can be cut into cubes for serving.

Parsley Jelly

Just cover a big bunch of parsley with water, add the peel of a lemon and boil for an hour. Strain off the liquid and add the juice of 3 lemons and to every cupful add a cup of sugar. Boil the liquor, testing for setting as for jam, putting droplets onto a cold plate. Put into little pots to set and store in a cool place. Eat your jelly with fish, veal or chicken.

Vegetable Goose *(Surrey, 18th-century)*

"Soak half a pound of bread crumbs in cold water, squeeze them nearly dry and mash them. Mix in one onion chopped small, one dessertspoonful chopped parsley and herbs, one ounce of butter, pepper and salt to taste. Put in a buttered dish and bake in a good oven for about one hour."

ROSEMARY

"cheerful rosemarie" — Spenser.

A sprig of rosemary, strangely aromatic, flavours soups, stews and roasted meat especially lamb, veal, pork and chicken. The Italians often cook their potatoes with rosemary.

Rosemary Hair Rinse

Cover a bunch of rosemary with water and simmer for ¾ of an hour.

SHAW AND THE FLOWER GIRLS

A sculptor king of Cyprus fell in love with his own creation, a statue of a woman. Aphrodite answered his prayer by giving it life. The king was called Pygmalion. Bernard Shaw's Pygmalion is Higgins, professor of phonetics, who turns the Covent Garden flower girl Eliza into "My Fair Lady". In the play she is first seen during a rain storm late at night in the portico of St Paul's, Inigo Jones's church in Covent Garden. Shaw sees her as not at all a romantic figure: "her little sailor hat of black straw has long been exposed to the dust and soot of London and has seldom if ever been brushed." Shaw gives her dirty hair, shoddy clothes, disintegrating boots; she is in need of a wash, in poor condition generally and has bad teeth. From Shaw's introduction to the play it seems likely that he was more interested in phonetics than in the flower-girls of Covent Garden. Indeed Eliza's first speech begins: "Ow, eez ye-ooa san is e? Wal, fewd dan y'd e-ooty bawmz a mather should 'eed how bettern . . . ." The lavish production of "My Fair Lady" as a film included a reconstruction of St Paul's Church on the set in Hollywood. Shaw died a wealthy man and left most of his money to found a new phonetic alphabet for the English language.

At the time of the Market moving to Nine Elms, Battersea, in 1974, there was a new production of "Pygmalion" running at the Albery Theatre, St Martin's Lane, with Diana Rigg as the flower girl.

Old English Toad-in-the-Hole

Toad-in-the-hole is English sausages cooked in Yorkshire pudding or egg batter. A little of the batter is set by putting it for a few minutes in a hot oven and the sausages are laid on this and then covered with the rest of the batter. Cook them in the oven for half an hour, and then turn the oven to a low setting in order to finish off the cooking for a further half hour.

The actress Diana Rigg has suggested a sauce for toad-in-the-hole. Finely slice and fry in oil or butter ½ lb of onions until soft and golden. Add 1 lb of skinned tomatoes, salt, pepper and rosemary. Cook until thick and pour over the toad before serving.

Flower girls, 1876

SAVORY

Winter and summer savory looks rather like thyme but has a sharper, more peppery tang. A leaf or two may be cooked with broad beans; this is one of the secrets of French cooking. Try it with lamb or pork and added to poultry stuffings. Relieve the pain of a bee sting by rubbing savory on the affected part.

SAGE

"Why should a man die who has sage in his garden?" Anon.

A Mediterranean herb brought to England by the Romans. It has been used for flavouring cheese, tea, wine, cream and even tobacco. The most popular poultry stuffing in England today is sage and onion. Sage flavours vegetable, egg and cheese dishes well; it also whitens the teeth and has a reputation for darkening hair.

Sage and Onion Stuffing *(from Mrs Beeton)*

"Take 4 large onions, 10 sage leaves, ¼ lb breadcrumbs, 1½ oz butter, salt and pepper to taste, and 1 egg. Peel the onions, put them into boiling water, let them simmer for 5 minutes or rather longer, and just before they are taken out, put in the sage leaves for a minute or two to take off their rawness. Chop both these very fine, add the bread, seasoning and butter, and work the whole together with the yolk of an egg, when the stuffing will be ready for use. It should be rather highly seasoned, and the sage leaves should be very finely chopped. Many cooks do not parboil the onions in the manner just stated, but merely use them raw, but the stuffing then is not nearly so mild, and, to many tastes, its strong flavour would be very objectionable. When made for a goose, a portion of the liver of the bird, simmered for a few minutes and very finely minced is frequently added to this stuffing; and where economy is studied, the egg and butter may be omitted.

This should be sufficient for 1 goose, or a pair of ducks."

TARRAGON

There is a special aroma to French tarragon. It flavours chicken or stuffing for turkey, also fish, veal and green vegetable soups. When obtainable I can use a lot of this delicate stuff without tiring of the taste.

Pot Roast Chicken with Tarragon

Season the inside of a roasting chicken with salt, pepper, ½ oz butter and 3 or 4 sprigs of tarragon. Truss its legs together to close the inside. Dry the skin and rub butter on it. Heat oil and butter in a casserole on top of the stove and brown the chicken all over. Avoid breaking the skin. Remove the chicken. Cook an onion and a chopped carrot together with some salt and 4 sprigs of fresh tarragon in the same oil for 5 minutes. Set the chicken on the vegetables and baste it. Put a tight-fitting lid on the casserole and roast in a pre-heated moderate oven until the drumsticks can be moved in their sockets (1-1½ hours).

THYME

"A strong infusion, drank as tea, is pleasant, and a very effectual remedy for head-ache, giddiness, and other disorders of that kind; and a certain remedy for the troublesome complaint, the nightmare."

Thyme is used to flavour soups, meat stews, stuffings, and some vegetables such as mushrooms, courgettes, aubergines and onions.

Herb sellers, 1876

BOW STREET & THE FIELDINGS

In the 1730s Fielding wrote a series of satires and bawdy farces for Drury Lane. "He would have thrown his work into the fire if meat could have been got without money, and money without scribbling" wrote a friend. In 1748 he was appointed magistrate & chief justice of Westminster & moved to Bow Street, then "an abode of thieves, prostitutes & unsuccessful authors." Here he wrote part of Tom Jones.

London's population doubled to 1 million between 1700 & 1800. A quarter of these were illiterate paupers. Gin offered cheap oblivion, the roads were infested with highwaymen & crime was at an all-time peak. The old system of justice, administered by unpaid gentry, was no longer able to cope.

Jonathan Wild, "Thief Taker General," flourished "finding" & selling back property he had stolen himself. He was said to be the original of Peachum in the Beggars Opera. Executed in 1725, he picked the chaplain's pocket while the last rites were being read, & died with the priest's bottle-screw in his hand.

"a proper Charlie!"

In Covent Garden, armed bands of pickpockets fell upon theatregoers & were more than a match for the old "Charlies," the watchmen.

Henry Fielding was outstandingly honest & efficient in a corrupt profession

"I reduced an income of £500 p.a. of the dirtiest money on earth to £300" wrote Fielding "Had the whole sum gone to my clerk, as it ought, he would be but ill-paid for sitting almost 16 hours in the 24 in the most naus-eous as well as unwholesome air in the universe, which hath in his case corrupted a good constitution without contaminating his morals". This ain broke Fielding's own health

Before he died in 1754, Fielding drew up the plan to establish the Bow Street Runners. The first 6 were appointed by his blind half-brother John. A forerunner of the C.I.D., they were renowned for their skill in solving difficult cases. They travelled all over the country & even abroad. Armed patrols were formed to police the streets at night. The Runners were replaced by Sir Robert Peel's "Bobbies" in 1828

The dashing young Lieutenant Hack-man fell in love with Lord Sand-wich's mistress Miss Reay. She remained faithful to her londly lover & bore him 9 children. Hackman took holy orders but was unable to forget her. In 1779 he shot her dead as she left Covent Garden Theatre. She was then 45. Hackman failed in his attempt to kill himself, was apprehended by Sir John Field-ing & exec-uted at Tyburn.

In 1769 you could still be hanged for stealing five shillings

A clergyman, O wicked one! In Covent Gar-den, shot her. No time to cry Upon her God! Tis hoped he's Not forgot her

THE SIGNIFICATION OF VEGETABLES WHICH APPEAR IN DREAMS

Taken from Richard Folkard's Plant Lore, *1884.*

CUCUMBERS
To see cucumbers in a dream denotes that you will speedily fall in love. Or, if you are not in love, then you will marry the object of your affection.
DANDELION
To see dandelions in your dreams betokens misfortune, and deceit on the part of your loved ones.
GARLIC
To dream that you are eating garlic denotes that you will discover hidden secrets and meet with some domestic jar. To dream there is garlic in the house is lucky.
LETTUCES
To dream of lettuces is said to portend trouble, and difficulty in the management of your affairs.
MUSHROOMS
To dream of mushrooms denotes fleeting happiness: to dream you are gathering them, fickleness in lover or consort.
NETTLES
To be stung by nettles in a dream means vexation and disappointment. To dream you are gathering them, happiness, approval and concord.
OLIVES
To dream of olives portends concord, liberty and dignity.
PARSLEY
If you dream that you are picking parsley, it portends that you will be crossed in love. If, on the other hand, you dream that you are eating it, you will shortly hear good news.
PUMPKINS
To dream of pumpkins is a very bad omen.
TURNIPS
To dream of turnips means fruitless toil.

The old overcrowded market, 1812

"MR EDITOR, — I much wish to know whose duty it is to clear away the filth of Covent Garden Market; for the negligence shown either by the Duke of Bedford's servants, or else by the respective owners of the stalls in the market, in not daily clearing away the putrid vegetables, and other impurities, which so offensively surround the same, as also the streets adjacent, particularly James and Southampton streets, is a disgrace in a country like ours. Perhaps this hint may be the means of bringing the birch-broom and pail rather oftener into play than they hitherto have been, and at the same time oblige your constant reader, H.H.M."

John Bull, *Wednesday, 8 August 1821*

COVENT GARDEN MARKET.

One of the greatest improvements of the Metropolis which has yet been projected, has till now remained unnoticed, though the plan is fully matured, and the execution will probably be, not only commenced, but completed at no very distant day.

It is intended to re-build the whole of Covent-garden Market, on one uniform and original plan.

At the extremities of the east and west fronts, four lodges, being each one story high, and consisting of two rooms, are to be erected. The two at the eastern end, as also those of the western end, will be connected by a terrace, sustained by doric columns formed of granite. On the terraces, it is proposed to expose flowers and fruits for sale, which are to be displayed in such order as will, it is presumed, render the place of their exhibition an attractive promenade.

The ground floors of the lodges will be made coffee or liquor shops, in lieu of those now existing in the market.

From the ends of each terrace, a conservatory, running from east to west, will be established. These will be covered in with glass, warmed with flues, and otherwise so disposed that the most delicate plants may be preserved in them, at all seasons of the year.

A middle building, extending from terrace to terrace, will occupy the centre of this market. Under this, cellars will be constructed, which may be let, independently or in connection with the shops contiguous. The whole of the upper part of this building, which rises in the model above the other erections, will be thrown into a hall, designed to be occupied with permanent standings along the sides, for the sale of fruits, vegetables, &c.

Nearly opposite Great Russell-street, and in a correspondent part of the western colonnade, there will be a public staircase leading to the hall, and to the terraces over the colonnades, from which there will be entrances to the conservatories.

Each of the terraces will be 145 feet in length by 28. By means of these and the hall, it is calculated that an accession of space, of 13,000 square feet, will be gained. The roof of the hall will be slated; the other buildings will be covered with zinc, with the exception of the conservatory, which, as we have already stated, will be glazed at the top. The whole arrangement is such as to afford the commodities brought to market greater protection against the weather than can now be obtained, while as much scope will be given for casualty business as heretofore.

The disposition of the plan is such as to be highly favourable to ventilation. The colonnades beneath the terraces will have every advantage of being in the open air, while they will offer a refreshing shade in the summer, and shelter from the rain in the inclement season of the year.

It is understood this great improvement will be effected at the sole expense of his Grace the Duke of Bedford. An Act of Parliament must first be obtained, but as no opposition can be anticipated, that circumstance will interpose little delay. The pillars, and various other parts of the proposed erections, can be prepared elsewhere, so that, when once the building is commenced, it may be expected to proceed with great rapidity. Mr. Fisher, his Grace's solicitor, is the author of the plan, which, whether we consider it as one merely ornamental, or look at it with a view to the more substantial merits connected with giving increased facilities and superior accommodation to the traders who resort to the market, reflects great credit on the inventor.

Newspaper report from the 1820s about the new market proposals

Part of the new market, 1831

"*A fountain has been erected, at the cost of the Duke of Bedford, on the Terrace at Covent Garden-market, between the two conservatories. It is not very large, but the design is handsome; seven or eight small jets of water spring from a circle, in the centre of which is a larger jet. The circle is composed of lotus leaves on the top of a vase, and the water falls into a patera of an elegant form, where it overflows, and trickles down into a basin formed with a fine bold curve, and made of polished Devon granite, which is the material of which the whole design is composed. This fountain will prove, in warm weather — should we ever be favoured with any — a most agreeable addition to the charms of the Terraces where the conservatories contain a fine collection of plants, both exotic and indigenous, many of which are in full flowers.*"
Observer, *22 March 1831.*

Floral Hall, 1860

SALADS

"Sallets (are) ready at hand, and easily dress'd, requiring neither Fire, Cost nor Attendance."

So John Evelyn had written in *Acetaria* of 1699: Queen Catherine, nearly two hundred years earlier had not found any sallets "ready at hand". So little were vegetables cultivated or gardening understood in the year 1509 that Queen Catherine could not procure a salad until Henry sent to the Netherlands and engaged a gardener to come over to raise the proper articles here. Soon gardens were full of "salletings" not only lettuce, cucumber, radish, mustard, cress, watercress, celery, beetroot, onions and "love apples" but a great many salad plants that were rarely used today. A sorrel bed was a common thing. Evelyn observed "sorrel imparts so grateful a quickness to the salad that it should never be left out". Chervil, purslane, burnet, lambs lettuce were to be found, and small mustard, tarragon, dandelion and several others. Unfortunately it is rare to find anyone who bothered to write down any formal recipes.

This excerpt is from *The English Hus-wife* by Gervase Markham (1615). It gives "a most complete method to compound an excellent sallet and which indeed is usual at great feasts, and upon Princes tables . . . Take a good quantity of blauncht Almonds, and with your shredding knife cut them grosly; then take as many Raisyns and the stones pickt out, as many figges shred like the Almonds, as many Capers, twice as many olives, and as many currants as of all the rest, cleane washt; a good handful of the small tender leaves of red Sage and Spinach, mix all these well together with a good store of Sugar, and lay them in the bottom of a great dish, then put unto them Vinegar and Oyle, and scrape more Sugar over all; then take Oranges and Lemons, and paring away the outward pills, cut them into their slices, then will those slices cover the sallat all over; which done, the thinne leafe of the red Coleflowre, and with them cover the oranges and lemons all over, then over those red leaves lay another course of Olives and the slices of well pickled coucumbers, together with the very inward heart of your Cabbage Lettice, cut into slices, then adorne the sides of the dish and the top of the Sallat with slices of Lemons and Oranges, and so serve it up."

Salad Dressings

"It takes four persons to make a salad dressing: a spendthrift to squander the oil, a miser to dole out the vinegar, a wise man to dispense the salt, a madman to stir."
                                                                                                Spanish saying.

"The greens and herbs were carefully chosen. All should fall into their place like the notes in music, in which there should be nothing harsh or grating." So wrote John Evelyn in 1699. To continue the simile, if the salad is music the dressing should act as a good conductor, bringing out the best in every part while blending the whole as one composition.

A salad should look beautiful but not be just decoration nor be overfull of an excess of exotic trimmings.

A simple vinaigrette sauce is a good basic dressing for nearly every salad.

A good mayonnaise goes with fish salad or the heavier root vegetables.

A Butter Dressing For Salads

Melt butter and when it is hot, but not brown, stir into it some crushed garlic, salt and pepper. Pour this mixture, while still hot, over lettuce, watercress, endive, sorrel, dandelion or similar leafy salad.

Yogurt Salad Dressing

Yogurt can be used as a dressing just as it is, it is improved if it is varied to suit a particular salad; flavours can be added such as a little mayonnaise, chopped chives, mint, parsley, onion, olives, nutmeg or garlic.

Salad Dressing Without Oil

Mix together half a teaspoon of made English mustard, 2 teaspoons of vinegar, a teaspoonful of chopped tarragon, basil or chives, the same of sugar or honey, half a clove of crushed garlic and the yolk of a hard-boiled egg. Stir in milk or cream. The eggwhite looks pretty sprinkled as decoration on the salad.

A Mixed Raw Vegetable Salad

Use carrot, turnip, celeriac, Jerusalem artichoke, kohlrabi, beetroot, the hearts of red and white cabbage, the hearts of Brussels sprouts, radish and sea kale.
    To make this salad easily digestible, grate the ingredients finely. However, it does look more pleasing if the vegetables are carefully cut small and then blanched. Allow plenty

of either vinaigrette, a cream dressing or mayonaise, because the vegetables will absorb a great deal.

Apple Salad *(from an 18th-century Sussex manuscript)*

"Two cupfuls of sour apple, half a cupful of celery, half a cupful of English walnuts, two tablespoonfuls of salad dressing, one cupful of whipped cream, one teaspoonful of sugar, salt and pepper."

Avocado Salad

Peel two ripe avocados, chop the flesh into cubes and sprinkle with lemon. Mix in some finely chopped onion and some vinaigrette. Mayonnaise is probably too heavy for the delicately flavoured and already rich avocado pear.

Green Bean Salad

French beans, young runner beans, bobby beans, young broad beans or in fact any beans or peas that are tender enough to eat complete with pods, make excellent salad when blanched. Sometimes they have such a good taste that they need only olive oil.

Purple Broccoli Salad

Blanch the broccoli until tender but still crunchy, drain immediately and arrange on a flat dish. Dress it about ten minutes before serving with a vinaigrette sauce made with lemon instead of vinegar to which some crushed garlic has been added.

Carrots

The best way of all to eat carrots is to grate them, perhaps with other roots or a coleslaw, and serve with just a little dressing of lemon, oil, salt, pepper and parsley. Carrots cut in thin strips lengthways are refreshing to eat and can be served with pieces of celery hearts for people to eat before a meal.

Cauliflower Salad

The flowerets, sliced thinly, may be eaten raw with a thin cream dressing. Cauliflower may also be grated and mixed with other vegetables. It is good undercooked and arranged around the side of a dish with some different salad in the centre. With a young cauliflower almost the whole can be used in salad. With the tougher, old ones, the discarded parts can be finely sliced and used in stews or soups in the place of turnips.

Celeriac Salad

Raw celeriac peeled and cut into long shreds makes a good *crudité* for hors d'oeuvre or to serve with drinks. Another method suitable for celeriac, salsify or kohlrabi is to cook the roots, slowly as for beetroot, and then peel and slice them. Serve cold with mayonnaise or vinaigrette.

Coleslaw

Grate or finely chop white Dutch cabbage, mix the pieces with mayonnaise or vinaigrette. Chopped carrots, currants and nuts can be added.

Cucumber Salad

Thinly-sliced cucumber is very good if prepared the day before required and left in French dressing to marinade in the refrigerator.

Dandelion and Sorrel

In early spring dandelion leaves can be eaten as salad mixed with a few chopped sorrel leaves. They have a bitter taste and should be dressed with vinaigrette just before serving, as with lettuce.

Endive Salad

Endive is used much like lettuce in salad or as a salad on its own. Endive leaves with chopped apple, nuts and currants with a vinaigrette dressing make an excellent winter salad.

Endive Salad *(19th-century manuscript from Middlesex)*

Take some fine white endives, carefully wash and drain them, and lay them in a salad bowl. Chop some shallots, wash them in several waters, and squeeze out the water in a cloth. Add them to the endive, together with some chopped tarragon, chervil and burnet. Season with thin mayonnaise sauce, and add two finely chopped Chili capsicums.

Fennel

The strong aniseed taste of fennel needs strong tasting partners, say radishes or watercress, a sprinkling of mint and a hint of garlic and some lemon juice instead of vinegar to mix with oil, salt and pepper.

Leek Salad

Use the smallest leeks. Take plenty because they shrink. Use the white part with just a little green. Boil them, allow to cool, arrange carefully, dress with a slightly sharp dressing and serve them really cold.

Mushroom Salad

Wash, drain and finely slice ½ lb of young firm mushrooms. Sprinkle them with lemon juice, salt, pepper and some olive oil and perhaps a little garlic. After at least ten minutes, sprinkle with parsley and serve. As an hors d'oeuvre try them with anchovies.

Pressed Salad

This macrobiotic recipe claims to render raw food more easily digestible. It is thus recommended for the old and very young. Any vegetable can be prepared by this method. In winter, a salad could be a watercress and cabbage, or for instance, carrots and endive. Cut the vegetables up finely, even shred them, add salt and cover with a plate. Place a weight on the plate. Under pressure the action of the salt on the vegetables will release a certain amount of juice. Save this for soups, sauces or a drink. After perhaps an hour or so, depending on the vegetable, your salad is ready to serve.

Pan Bagna

For a picnic a thick French loaf is cut down the centre lengthways and soaked in oil, preferably olive oil, for an hour. Strain off the oil, rub the bread with garlic, spread one of the halves with ratatouille and cover with the other half before putting it under a weighted dish. Prepare it the day before the picnic.

Rice or Potato with Beetroot Salad

When rice or potatoes are marinated with beetroot in a vinaigrette the whole takes on a glorious beetroot scarlet and make a very fine salad.

Salad Brittany *(from M. Chion at Rules Restaurant)*

Boil until just tender some carrots, turnips, potatoes and beetroot. Rinse them separately in cold water and then dice each finely. Chop, again finely, some spring onion and radish. Mix all these together with a mayonnaise containing some mustard and plenty of finely-chopped tarragon.

Salade Niçoise

There is no exact recipe for a Salade Niçoise. Lettuce hearts, hard boiled eggs, olives, anchovies, tomato and tuna fish are the most usual ingredients. It should be a fairly simple tasty mixed salad dressed at the last minute with a vinaigrette sauce containing garlic.

Salsify or Scorzonera

The leaves of both plants, when young, make good green salads. The roots, when boiled, drained, allowed to cool and served in vinaigrette also make a pleasant salad.

Spinach Cooked as Salad

Three pounds of raw spinach serves about 4 people. Blanch the spinach using no water except what is left on the leaves after washing. Drain it and chop it a little and, when cool, put on some dressing with lemon juice in it. You can add some sliced or diced boiled potato. If you press the spinach into moulds before putting it to chill, you can turn it out and serve it on a lettuce leaf or surrounded by tomatoes or triangles of hot, buttered toast.

Spring Onions Vinaigrette

Wash and trim spring onions and tie them in a bunch like asparagus. Cook until tender in boiling salted water. Then leave to cool and serve with herb vinaigrette, perhaps chopped chervil and tarragon.

Tomato Salad with Yogurt and Cream

Peel some small tomatoes, and leaving them whole, spread them out, onto a pretty dish. Pour over mixture of yogurt, cream, tarragon, basil, salt and pepper.

Tomato Salad Provençale

Traditionally a mortar and pestle is used to pound together garlic, olive oil and parsley complete with stalks. This mixture is mixed with the scooped-out flesh of tomatoes and stuffed back into the tomatoes. Leave for an hour or two, for the flavours to sink in, before serving.

Winter Salad

Diced beetroot is dressed with highly-seasoned oil and vinegar. Celery, cut into thin small sticks, is dressed separately with a milder, sweeter dressing and then arranged on and around the beetroot. These ingredients combine well to accompany roast chicken or turkey.

Winter Salad *(19th-century manuscript from Middlesex)*

"Cut up some endive and celery, add two tablespoonfuls of russet apples, cut into dice. Stir well and cover these with half a pound of grated nuts, and mix mayonnaise sauce with the whole."

Winter Salad *(18th-century manuscript from Surrey)*

"Take some white haricot beans, French beans, potatoes, beetroot, and onions. Blanch all the vegetables separately, cool and drain them. Chop the onions, and put them in the corner of a cloth; dip this in cold water, and press the water out of the onion. Do this two or three times, which will render the onion more digestible. Cut the potatoes and beetroots in half inch discs. Put all into a salad-bowl, adding some chopped chervil; season with salt, pepper, oil, and vinegar, and mix the whole well."

A CONVERSATION IN THE GARDEN ON THE SITE OF ST PAUL'S CHURCHYARD, JUNE 1974

Mr Hatch: *I always say that it is for my sins that I work at a church, for there is no harder job than being a verger at a church. You have got to have eyes everywhere – if it's not adults, it's children. Last Sunday there were three boys here smashing down the flowers that had taken three months to grow. At their age I was at Sunday School learning how to behave . . . . Now you ask me what you want to know?*

I have always wondered what that box is, in the corner.

That is the Beadle's hut, where the Beadle used to have a badge of office and his particular job was to watch for body-snatchers. This place was one mass of graves. Somewhere round here it tells you when these graves were deconsecrated and, well, you may be able to read it, I barely can and I can't remember those dates – I've got it written down somewhere . . . . The Rector of St Paul's was Simon Patrick, he became first Bishop of Ely. When the Plague was on he risked his life to stay, tending the sick and burying the dead. Instead of their being buried in one pit he buried everyone individually. Even if it was an unknown maid, an unknown child and all in his own handwriting you'll find it in the records of this church. The records are now in the library at Buckingham Palace Road.

The Plague, which spread everywhere, started round here somewhere (1664). It stopped about here, too, and I suppose it was Charley Two that appreciated the fact that the

*green vegetables coming from Surrey and all around by horse and cart stopped the
Plague from spreading so the King issued a Charter that there should be a coffee stall
there for the refreshment of drivers that brought the green food.*

At the beginning how did this church become a separate parish?

*It was originally a chapel attached to St Martin-in-the-Fields and then they wanted their
own parish. The Earl of Bedford was supported by a hundred local people who petitioned
the King. The Earl, as usual, won the day. But the Act, establishing Covent Garden as a
parish, took some time to happen because the Civil War came in between.*

*The entrance to the church was the other end. After the fire (1795) when the church
was burnt out the altar was brought back to its proper end — for the church had been
built back to front. The vaults here are still sealed up — we call it a crypt. But it isn't a
crypt until it is opened up and you can go into it. You can't yet, so the shape of things to
come is for it to be opened rather like St Martin's.*

Are there good things inside?

*Nobody knows . . . . there must be — there are tombs in there. I would imagine there
must be leaden coffins. In St Mary-le-Bow, bombed and rebuilt, they found not only
leaden coffins but basket coffins. Coffins used to be made of baskets — you didn't know
that did you?*

No.

They did. There is a sort of tin, or something, inside a basket.

When was that?

I wouldn't really know but it goes back to the Middle Ages.

When was this crypt sealed up?

The last burial was in 1857 . . . .

Your church has a tradition for being the actors' church?

*The association with actors began, as you may have read, when all the female roles
were taken by men. You have got all the streets around here named after actors: Kemble
Street, Macklin Street, Kean Street. Most of the theatrical profession lived in the Bow
Street-Drury Lane area.*

*There have been many quarrels about which is the actors' church. St Vedast in Foster
Row used to claim they were the actors' church. That goes back to the days when
performances were done in the open in Cheapside. So really in the ancient days they had
a certain claim.*

*Ellen Terry and her family lived overlooking this churchyard. Ben Webster and his wife
lived just up there . . . .*

What of the future here?

*I have known the church since 1914. I worked in this part of London as a youngster.
The rectory of this church used to be across the road in King Street. I expect you knew
that we had one Rector who was killed in the First World War, the Reverend Moss. There
was an aerial torpedo dropped from a plane. He was seeing people into the shelter by*

Odhams in Long Acre. He was killed with all the others. He was buried in Finchley. One of his sons was also killed in the War and his name is on the First War Memorial inside the church. But this doesn't serve as a parish church any longer because we have no resident parishioners. I think actually we have got two. As a parish church this has ceased. I would imagine that in the shape of things to come that this church will be used for music and the arts. We have had nearly everything in here — we have had Godspell, *we've had art exhibitions, concerts. There could be a small chapel at the side for worship. As long as the church is preserved — and the garden — I am quite happy. I had a neighbour coming to us the other night complaining that the Charing Cross Hospital was going to be turned into a home for dossers. She was very indignant. She was going to write to her MP to the Council. But I said "Well, you're much too late — people have protested about these things for months — you wouldn't even read the literature I offered you. There were meetings, the community centre!. . . . So we go on.*

"COVENT-GARDEN MARKET. In consequence of the annoyances to which ladies have recently been subjected when visiting this market by the vexatiously importunate applications of the basket-women for jobs, the Steward of the market yesterday caused public notice to be given that from and after Saturday next inclusive, the by-laws would be strictly enforced, and the basket-women and porters kept in the places assigned to them, nor allowed to enter the principal walks, unless called to a job."
Newspaper report, 2 April 1835

Entrance to the new market, 1834

"COVENT GARDEN

French beans were 5s per 100 to-day, and cucumbers (forced) 10s to 16s per brace. The supply of fruits and vegetables was again good. Trade very moderate. Pines 5s to 9s 8d per lb.; asparagus 3s to 12s per hundred. Other fruits, etc. etc., remain without any alterations in prices from this day se'nnight."
Morning Chronicle, *9 February 1835*

THEATRICAL LIFE IN COVENT GARDEN

Charles the Second granted a Patent to Killigrew in 1663 to open the Theatre Royal, Drury Lane, creating the first link between Covent Garden & theatrical life. The King's Men, wore special livery & took the Oath of Allegiance as members of the Royal Household.

Female parts were for the first time performed by women. Evelyn complained that the actresses were "inflaming severall young noblemen & gallants. They became their whores, & to some their wives, to the reproch of their noble families, and the ruin both of Body & Soule."

When the Earl of Ilchester's daughter married a handsome young actor from Drury Lane in 1764, London was outraged. "I could not have believed Lady Susan would have stooped so low" wrote Walpole "It is the completion of disgrace—even a footman were preferable"

In 1732, John Rich, a theatre owner, had a great commercial success with Gay's 'Beggar's Opera'. He built the Theatre Royal, Covent Garden, which soon became the chief rival to Drury Lane.

This Beggar's Opera hath made Gay rich & Rich gay.

Mackie

Restoration theatregoing was a pastime for men of fashion. Performances were at 3 in the afternoon. Gentry sat in the boxes or on the stage, their ladies masked to hide their blushes. Men of fashion sat in the pit to see & be seen, exchanging bons mots, rarely listening to the play. They paid no admission fee if they stayed for only one act. There was much trafficking with the orange girls who sold "oranges, lemons, sweetmeats, and no doubt other favours"

The 1809 Old Prices Riot. Refusing to accept a rise in seat prices, the public shouted the actors down on opening night & continued to riot & damage the theatre for the next 77 nights. Kemble, then manager, employed pugilists to fight the rioters in the pit & had many of the ringleaders arrested. Finally he was forced to reduce the pit prices to 3s 6d

Drury Lane Theatre has burned down 3 times, Covent Garden twice

In 1808, the Theatre Royal, Covent Garden was gutted. The £150,000 building was insured for only £35,000. Sheridan, who ran the theatre to support his political career, was ruined. Challenged for watching the fire calmly from the Piazza Coffee House, Sheridan replied "May not a man warm himself at his own fireside?"

The last great fire at Covent Garden was in 1856, when the theatre was sub-let for a season of spectaculars and melodramas. The impresario lost so much money that he was allowed to hold a fund-raising ball masqué on the last night. The ball was attended by "a sorry collection of riff-raff pretty far gone in drink", as one observer said. When the National Anthem was being played at 5.0 a.m., fire broke out & the theatre was totally destroyed.

The present Drury Lane Theatre was built in 1812, the Royal Opera House in 1858

FRUIT

APPLES

Introduced from Gaul into Britain by the Romans, some of the monasteries kept their orchards of apples throughout the Dark Ages and these apples kept their good reputation as a fruit. Henry VIII sent off to France for grafts which were brought back to Tenham in Kent where an orchard was established. Kent today is Britain's most important apple growing area.

The two most favoured apples are Cox's Orange Pippin and the Bramley Seedling. Mr Cox, a retired brewer, planted two pips in a flower pot. One became the Cox's Orange Pippin tree and the other Cox's Pomona and every Cox's apple comes from grafts made with cuttings that come originally from the trees Mr Cox grew in 1830.

A girl planted an apple pip in the garden of a Nottinghamshire cottage in 1805 and she looked after the tree until it bore fruit. During the following fifty years she gave away many cuttings to friends and neighbours. Eventually a local nurseryman asked permission to distribute the cuttings commercially and was told he could do so provided they bore the family name of Bramley. The original tree still exists.

The marketing arrangements for apples are so developed that apples are available all the year round, coming either from storage or from imports. This introduction of grading seems to have led to a loss in their eating qualities, flavour, juiciness and so forth. Indeed the European Economic Community (EEC) standards for fresh apples and pears require that for extra quality (there are four classes: Extra, I, II, III) the fruit must be typical in shape, development and colouring; the only mention of taste is that all qualities must be "free from any foreign smell or taste" (the use of the word foreign is about the only jokey thing in these gloomy EEC documents).

Buttered Apples

This is a very simple and absolutely delicious way of cooking apples. Bramleys are best because they turn fluffy when cooked. Prepare and slice 1 lb of apples into a buttered ovenproof dish, dot 1 oz of butter over the apples, sprinkle 2 tablespoons of brown sugar over and place 2 pieces of lemon peel on top.

Leave the dish uncovered in a medium oven for about half an hour. The apples are good enough to eat without cream or custard.

Buttered Apples on Bread

This is easier than making pie or crumble. Just peel (optional) and core the number of apples you need and put each apple on a round ½ inch thick piece of bread with all the crust taken off. Put into each apple as much butter and sugar in equal quantities as it will hold, together with a piece of lemon peel. Cook them on a buttered tray in a moderately hot oven. Before serving put a teaspoonful of red currant jelly in each apple.

Apple Cake *(from an 1840 manuscript)*

"Boil 1 to 2 lbs of sugar in a pint of water till it is reduced to half then add 2 lbs of apples cored and sliced very thin with the rinds of 2 lemons until it boils but take care that it is not burnt then add the juice of the 2 lemons boil 2 minutes oil your molds and put the apples into them. It will keep good for a month."

Apple Charlotte

Cut thin slices of bread and remove all the crusts. Butter them well on both sides and line a pie dish or oven proof basin with them. Prepare and slice apples thinly and pack them into the lined dish with sprinkles of demerara sugar and a little grated lemon rind between each layer. Cover the top layer with breadcrumbs and demerara sugar and generously dot with butter. Bake until the top is golden brown (1 hour). As a *tour de force*, the Charlotte may be willing to turn out onto a plate to amaze your family and friends!

Apples Stewed in Cider

Slice the apples, one for each person, and put them in a saucepan or fireproof dish. Sprinkle with brown sugar and add at least a dessert spoonful of cider for each apple. Bake covered in a moderate oven for half an hour, then baste and cook for a few more minutes. Before cooking you can dot with butter if you are not going to serve it with cream, mix in currants or flavour with either cloves, cinnamon or lemon, depending on how tasty you expect the apples to be. Really good apples are best with sugar alone.

Apple Crumble

This is an English dish much admired by foreigners. Crumble topping is simply the ingredients for a short pastry, mixed together but without any water. It is quicker and tastier to make a crumble than a pie. I often set out to make the latter but am never disappointed when I am rushed or distracted and end up with a crumble. I make crumble with all the sugar in the crust to get a contrast with the sharp taste of apple. Some cooks put most of the sweetening into the fruit and others half and half. Each to your own taste.

6 oz flour, 3 oz butter, 1 lb large cooking apples, 1 oz sugar.

Rub the fat into the flour and the sugar with fingertips until it has the consistency of fine breadcrumbs. Prepare and slice the apples, put them into a pie dish and moisten with water. Cover the apples with the crumble mix and press down with the flat of the hand. Bake until deep golden brown, in a hot oven (20-30 minutes.) It tastes better eaten after cooling down a little.

Apple Crumble Pudding

This is a superior version of apple crumble and is a recipe from Mrs Eve Patrick who lives in Drury Lane. Sprinkle cinnamon in the mixture and powdered cloves on the apple. Put layers of apple and crumble mixture in a buttered, oven-proof dish, finishing with crumble layer. Pour over the pudding 4 oz of orange juice and 2 oz of lemon juice, sprinkle the grated fruit rinds on top. For a really lush finish, pour over 2 fl oz of calvados and, after baking in a moderate oven for 1 hour, serve with cream.

Apple Dumplings

For 4 medium-sized cooking apples, use 6 oz self-raising flour, 3 oz shredded suet, jam, brown sugar and dried fruit.

Mix the suet evenly into the flour and moisten with enough water to make it into a normal dough consistency. Roll this suet paste out fairly thinly and cut it into quarters Peel and core the apples and fill the hole with the sugar, jam and fruit. Completely envelop each apple in paste and put them on to a greased baking tin to bake in a medium oven for about 1 hour.

Apple Fritters

Make a stiff fruit batter and have ready a deep frying pan or a saucepan with oil or fat about ½ inch deep. Peel, core and slice the apples about ¼ inch thick. Dip each slice in the batter and make sure that it is completely coated. Have the oil hot and fry each piece for about 5 minutes or until golden brown. Drain on kitchen paper and serve them immediately with castor sugar sprinkled over them.

Mousse à la Russe

"Make an apple sauce by gently cooking apples to a purée with some butter, lemon juice and sugar. Fold one cup of apple into the stiffly-beaten whites of 5 eggs. Pile the mixture into a pyramid in an oven-proof dish. Sprinkle with granulated sugar and bake at gas 2, 300F for 40 minutes. Serve with a bowl of cream, whipped thick but not stiff."

Nostalgia is two tiny shops in Bedfordbury selling clothes of the 1920s, 30s and 40s. Sharon Smeed, the exotically-attired young owner, found this recipe in a *Tante Marie* of 1924. Like many of the clothes, this mousse is pale and beautiful.

Chinese Glazed Apples or Drawn Thread Apples

Caramelize a mixture of brown sugar, oil and a little honey. Make apple fritters then dip them into the hot sugar mixture. Pile them in a sticky mound and take them to the table, with a scattering of sesame seeds over them if possible. Before eating, use a fork to dip each one into cold water; this turns the outside to cold crunchy toffee while the inside remains a hot juicy fritter.

Apple Pie

Prepare and slice about 1-1½ lbs apples into a pie dish that is small enough to be then quite full, sprinkle with water to moisten the apples, with about 1 oz of sugar and dust on ½ teaspoon of cinnamon or a few cloves. Roll out some short pastry and then put it on as a lid by rolling the pastry up on the pin and then unrolling it over the top of the dish. Trim the edges with a knife and then press them to the dish with a fork. Make a slot in the the middle with a knife and for a glossy golden effect brush the top with beaten egg and milk. Bake in a medium oven for about 40 minutes. Serve hot or cold with or without cream, custard or cream cheese.

A cheese pastry can make a good crust for apple pie. Make the pastry in the usual way with 6 oz of flour, 2 oz of butter or shortening and 2 oz of grated cheddar cheese.

Scraped Apples *(from a manuscript book of 1840)*

"Take 1 lb of good eating apples, peel them and scrape or shred them finely with a sharp knife into a glass dish. Have ready, not too hot, a nice, two egg custard, flavoured with sugar and vanilla and pour this at once over the apples, as they discolour while exposed to the air. Let them be well covered with the custard. This is a most delicious and wholesome dish and will suit invalids."

Harengs Frais Ilmen

"Herrings with Apple Stuffing

For 4 people:

4 fresh unsalted herrings	½ onion
3 apples	5 oz sour cream
3 sweet-sour gherkins	salt and pepper

Bone the herrings and steam for approximately 5 minutes in Fond (stock or bouillon). Leave to cool. When cold, drain and fill the herring with slices of peeled apples, gherkins and onion rings.

To prepare the sauce, grate 2 apples and 2 gherkins, press till dry. Mix with sour cream. Season to taste. Cover with herrings with the sauce and serve with a salad."

This is a recipe contributed by Mr Santosh, the chef of the Inigo Jones Restaurant in Floral Street.

Apple Tart

Make a pastry in a buttered tart tin; fork a few holes in it. Peel 2 lbs of apples and save the peel; slice the apples finely and arrange them in 2 layers on the top of the pastry, sprinkle each layer with white sugar and squeeze over them a little lemon juice and a very small pinch of cinnamon if you like it. Bake in a moderate oven until the apples are golden and a little browned on top but soft and moist underneath (30 minutes). Prepare a glaze by heating together a couple of tablespoons of water, a tablespoon of sugar, the peel of the apple and a dessertspoon of brandy or cider.

For an alternative glaze, boil a tablespoonful of apricot jam with one of water and then strain.

Apple Turnovers

This is a good alternative to apple pie for picnics, and for people who like plenty of pastry. Make some shortcrust pastry and roll it quite thin. Cut circles out of it with a saucer. Peel core and slice ½ lb of apples, put the slices on to the rounds of pastry well over to one side, sprinkle with a little sugar and a cinnamon, moisten the edge of the pastry and fold it in half over the apple slices, pressing the edge firmly all round. Make a small hole in the top of each turnover, sprinkle with sugar and put them on to a greased baking tray to cook in a medium oven for about half an hour.

Mince Pies — a useful tip

The landlady, Mrs Margaret Elston, of the Crown and Anchor, Endell Street keeps the pub traditional, as the local and regular customers prefer it. Mrs Elston likes to cook English food at home. She reckons mince pies are lighter and better eating with a layer of sliced apple on top of the mincemeat, before the pastry top is put on. Brush the tops with egg and sprinkle with brown sugar.

Taffety Tart

Pastry for an 8-inch pie, 6 large cooking apples, 1 lemon, the rind grated, the pulp cut into small pieces, ½ lb of sugar and 2 oz butter.

Line the pie dish with pastry and arrange the apples in layers. Between each layer sprinkle the sugar and lemon rind and some of the chopped lemon. Dot with butter and cover with a top crust. Puncture to let the steam out. Bake in a moderate oven for 40 minutes.

APRICOT

Apricot Compôte

Cut in half and stone 2 lbs of apricots, heat up ½ pint of water, dissolve in it ¼ lb sugar, put in a vanilla pod and the apricots. Cook gently, until tender but not too soft. Take the apricots from the liquid and boil this until it is reduced to a fairly thick syrup. Pour this over the apricots and serve cold.

Baked Apricots

Cut 2 lbs of apricots in half, stone them and then make a mountain from the base of a baking dish. Heat up 2 tablespoons of water with 2 tablespoons of sugar and a vanilla pod or a ¼ teaspoon of extract. When the sugar is dissolved, pour the liquid over the apricots and place the dish in the centre of a low oven until the apricots are tender but not too soft (1 hour). Serve hot from the oven and surrounded by triangles of "eggy bread": bread put into a mixture of egg and milk and then fried in butter and sprinkled with sugar.

Apricot Tart

Line a buttered tart tin with thinly rolled short pastry; fork a few holes in it. On top of the pastry arrange apricots cut in half and stoned. Pack them in really tight as they will shrink with cooking. Sprinkle with 3 oz sugar per lb. Bake in a moderate oven for about ½ hour.

When the tart has cooled glaze it with any extra apricots stewed with a little sugar and water or a tablespoon of apricot jam boiled with a little water. A teaspoon of apricot brandy is a good addition to the glaze.

BÁNANAS

A conversation with Mr Forrester of Neal Street, June 1974

Mr Forrester: *There are three importers: Jamaica Producers are a Jamaican company dealing with Jamaican bananas; Elders and Fyffes bring bananas in from all over the world; and Geest deal mainly with bananas from Dominica. We are an agency for Fyffes and for Jamaica producers. We are small people by modern standards.*
  Are you going to move to the New Market at Nine Elms?
  We hope to. Our problem is a little more complicated. They haven't built us banana ripening rooms. We have only just realized that. We thought that under the terms of the Act they were going to provide people with facilities for carrying on their businesses if they were forcibly moved from here. We have problems over there that other people haven't got.
  Could you stay here?
  I don't think it is very likely. We don't run a delivery service, you see. Our customers are here in the Market. They have got to take the bananas away with their own transport.
  Is this a Market Authority warehouse?
  No. We sublet from a company who have a lease from the Mercers Company. As the situation is now, we are moving because the customers have been taken away.
  How much of the selling of bananas is to supermarkets?
  We don't do any supermarkets here at all. That is mainly left to the depots of the big importers. Ours is mainly small retail trade or to other wholesalers in the Market who haven't got any ripening facilities.
  When did you stop having those lovely wooden boxes?
  They have been on the way out for four or five years now because bananas don't come into the country on stems any more. They used to come in on a stem of bananas: six, seven or eight hands on a stem. And then they were cut here when they were ripened. But they are cut in Jamaica now and packed into cartons in Jamaica. We simply ripen them, turn them over, check the quality and the weights and then send them out again. Repack them and send them out again.
  Are there more and more bananas being sold all the time?
  No, less and less, because they have had certain problems growing them. In the growing countries they are in this drought belt that is going around the world. The West Indies and most of the growing countries have been hit by drought for the last two or three years. So, in fact, imports are fewer.
  In Italy or France bananas seem to cost as much as steak. Do you think that is going to come here? Do you see any connection between higher prices and the Common Market?

I don't think it's a question of the Common Market, is it? It's a question of travel becoming so easy that the whole world is becoming smaller. What affects one country one day is bound to affect others the next.

Do you think that prices will rocket up to those levels?

I think in the long run prices in this country will be similar to what they are anywhere in the world regardless of Common Markets or any other markets. Whether they will rocket up or come down I don't know but they are likely to do it all at the same time. With better refrigerated shipping and faster ships we may bring them from the far side of the world and then we will have a world stable price for bananas. Whether it be up or down will depend on what they grow elsewhere.

Banana Custard

Banana custard is simply bananas sliced into hot custard and eaten hot or cold. A little grated nutmeg on top is good if you like nutmeg.

To make an egg custard, 2 to 3 eggs with ¾ pint of milk, as little or much sugar as you like, a pinch of salt and vanilla pod or essence are stirred in a double saucepan over a gentle heat. Beat gently until the custard thickens and coats a spoon, then remove from the heat.

Banana Rum Cream

Bananas and rum combine well. Have ½ pint of cream chilled and mix 1 or 2 tablespoons of rum into it. Peel the bananas and slice them into the mixture and stir gently. Sprinkle with a pinch or two of powdered coffee or some grated dark chocolate.

Simple Recipes for Cooking Jamaica Bananas
by a Black Lady *(from a manuscript of 1870)*

"1. As a Vegetable, wholesome, and filling. Peel *green bananas,* boil them in salt and water until soft like potatoes. Are good mashed with butter and peppernut.

2. Fried Bananas. These are what children like. Ripe bananas, sliced lengthways, fried in lard. Eaten with either meat, or served with sugar sprinkled on them. A squeeze of lemon is an improvement.

3. Baked Bananas. Fit for the gods! Peel ripe bananas and place in a pie-dish. Sprinkle a little lemon juice over them (also sugar), half cover with water, bake for twenty minutes. When cool, serve with custard, cream or milk.

4. Banana Fritters. If well made are tip-top. Dip them whole or sliced in batter. Fry until crisp and light brown."

Banana Caramel

Peel and slice the bananas into quarters. Prepare a caramel sauce which is the consistency of thin cream. Simmer the bananas in the sauce until they just begin to soften and go floppy (2-5 minutes). Serve immediately with a little sauce and a good dollop of chilled cream.

Banana Fritters

Peel the bananas, cut them in half lengthways and then into quarters. Dip the pieces individually into batter and then put them one by one into a deep fryer. Fry until golden brown, drain on kitchen paper, sprinkle with castor sugar and serve hot with lemon.

BILBERRY

A small blue English summer berry, naturalized in the USA where the name is given to a number of different berries. In England it is found in woods and on hillsides, and has many local names, such as Wortleberries, Hurts in Surrey, Whinberries in the North and Wales, Blaeberries in Westmorland and Scotland. They are excellent in pies with apple or on their own and they make good jam.

Bilberry Fritters

Make an unsweetened batter. Add enough bilberries to make it quite thick. Drop fritters into ¼ inch deep oil or butter and cook as apple fritters. Drain them and sprinkle them generously with sugar before serving them hot.

"Now that the north and south sides of Covent-garden Market are completed, demolition has reached the centre: and the well-known row of shops, where so many of our readers have hung their eyes devouringly on early peas and asparagus, is now no more."
Newspaper report, October 1829.

BLACKBERRIES

The flavour, the scent, for me recalls the hotter summers that used to be, and the purple fingers and tongues with just a few heated blackberries to show at the bottom of the jar. With such a good flavour, their only fault is having so many pips. To remove the pips, heat up 1 oz of sugar per pound of fruit and then push them through on sieve. This procedure is rather tedious and you lose some half of the weight. If you really do not like the pips choose very large fruit with more flesh or use just a few blackberries mixed with apples.

Blackberry Pie

Make this in the same way as apple pie, replacing some or all of the apples with blackberries. No cinnamon or cloves are necessary.

Blackberry Pancakes

¼ lb of flour, about 2 tablespoons sugar, 1 egg, 1 cup blackberries, ½ oz butter and 2 cups milk.

Mix the flour, blackberries, sugar, egg yolk and milk together to form a batter. Melt the butter and stir it in, beat the egg white stiffly and add it to the mixture to make little omelette-like pancakes. Brown on both sides and serve them hot with vanilla ice-cream.

Blackberry and Apple Pudding

This is a hearty pudding and needs 6 oz self-raising flour, 3 oz shredded suet, 1 oz sugar, 1 lb fruit which is a mixture of peeled, cored and sliced apples with washed blackberries.
　　Mix the flour and shredded suet together, evenly and lightly. Moisten with water to a paste consistency. Divide the paste in two. Roll one half out until it is large enough to completely line a basin. Moisten the basin and line it with this rolled out paste. Roll out the other half of the dough to form a round lid for the basin.
　　Put the apples and the blackberries into the lined basin with sugar between the layers, add 2 tablespoons of water. Moisten the edge of the basin and firmly seal the dough lid in position. Cover the basin over the top and halfway down with metal foil, floured cloth or greaseproof paper and tie a string around the basin to hold it in place. Put the pudding basin into a saucepan, with a well fitting lid, surrounded but not covered by boiling water. Steam for at least 2 hours — longer will do it no harm, it is almost impossible to overcook the pudding but be careful that the water does not boil away.

BLACKCURRANTS

Blackcurrant Tart

Make short pastry and line an 8″ buttered flan dish. Fill the flan case with blackcurrants, picked over, washed and still damp. Add a good sprinkling of sugar. Bake in a hot oven for about 25 minutes.

For a pie:-

Cover the fruit with pastry and it may take a little longer to cook than the tart if you make it deeper.

Blackcurrant Jelly

Pick off stalks, wash the blackcurrants, weigh them, and put them into a saucepan with a measured capacity. Add 1½ pints of water for each pound of fruit. Crush the fruit, bring just to the boil and simmer for half an hour. Take off the heat and dissolve gelatine into the mixture, one ounce to the pint. Empty the saucepan into in a wetted mould and leave in a cool place to set.

For a clear jelly, strain the liquid off through a fine sieve or a cloth before adding the gelatine

Summer Pudding

For this dish, a famous and delicious English pudding, there is no exact recipe, since the idea of it is to use any of the soft summer fruits available. However it looks best with plenty of purple fruit, blackcurrants, blackberries and/or any mixture of them with redcurrants, whitecurrants, strawberries, raspberries and gooseberries.

Line a basin with crustless bread. Stew the fruit for a few minutes with just a little water, and some sugar added. When there is plenty of juice pour this and the fruit into the bread-lined basin which must be completely filled before covering with a bread lid. Put a plate and then a weight on top and leave it in a cool place overnight or for several hours at least.

Making this pudding, although very simple, calls for a nice judgement: there must be enough juice to soak right through the bread and colour it but the pudding must not be too sodden or it will collapse when it is turned out.

BLUEBERRIES

Small summer berries that make good pies, puddings, jams, jellies, sauces and preserves.

CHERRIES

There are over a hundred sorts of wild cherries, two main types of which are cultivated
and marketed. Because birds can eat all the cherries off a single, isolated tree, growing
cherries commercially has to be done on a large scale, so that man and bird can each have
a share; this perhaps is why only a few out of the many varieties are found in the Market.
The two main types of cherry are the sweet or the sour. Sweet cherries are unlikely to
gain anything by cooking so most attention here is given to the sour cherries. The most
important is the Morello cherry, either red or black. These make marvellous jam, and
the bitter-sharp taste of cooked Morellos contrasted with cream and say, chocolate
sponge, makes about the most delicious thing that I know of in the way of a
cream-filled, passionate sort of cake. Another sour cherry is the Damasca from which
Maraschino liqueur is made. The Amarello is a sour cherry that, when quite ripe,
can also be eaten uncooked as a dessert.

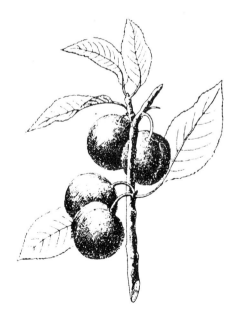

Stewed Cherries

For sour Morello cherries allow about 4 oz sugar per pound. Cook gently in a covered saucepan with just enough water to cover. When soft (10 minutes), cool and, if available, add some Kirsch or brandy. A more ambitious, more rewarding recipe is to just cover the cherries with claret, add the sugar and a pinch of cinnamon, poach slowly until soft (10 minutes), remove the cherries and reduce the liquid to a syrup. When it is cooking add a tablespoon of redcurrant jelly per pound of cherries and pour the syrup back over the cherries. Serve cold with cream.

Cherry Tart

Line a shallow tin with short pastry rolled thin and baked in a hot oven until golden brown. When cool spread thick cream or a cream filling over the crust and then cover with the cherries that have been stewed and stoned, and reduce the syrup until it is thick enough to use as a glaze.

CHINESE GOOSEBERRY

A furry brown egg-shaped fruit that is neither a gooseberry nor, today, usually Chinese, this is often marketed as "kiwi fruit" from New Zealand although it will grow in England. When cut in half it reveals jade green jelly-like flesh that is eaten without further preparation by the teaspoonful. Chill slightly before eating.

CRAB APPLE

The sour crab-apple makes excellent jams, jellies and preserves.

Crab Apple Jelly

6 lbs of crab-apples, 2 lemons and 1 lb of sugar to each pint of juice.

Wash and core the apples and cut them into quarters. Just cover them with water and boil for ¾ of an hour. Strain them and add 1 lb of sugar to each pint of juice. Boil them together for another ¾ of an hour stirring frequently, add the lemon juice just before the jelly is ready — test this by seeing if it jellies on a cold spoon. You may prefer to leave out the lemon juice and use cinnamon or cloves as a flavour, or indeed use no added flavour at all.

DATES

A date is an oblong berry with a grooved seed, the fruit of a palm tree. It comes to England, fresh or dried, from the desert regions of North Africa and Israel.

Date Moons

Chop ½ lb of stoned dates and mix into them about 6 oz of walnuts and 2 oz of candied ginger, all coarsely cut. Knead the mixture and roll it into sausages, use icing sugar to prevent sticking. Cut into thin slices and serve.

Nineteenth-century market scene

FIGS

When ripe just wash them and eat them raw, skins and all, but only eat a few at a time. It is quite smart to peel them and eat them with very thin slices of lean uncooked smoked ham as an hors d'oeuvre. For figs that are not in prime condition, peel them and pour over them very finely chopped crystallized ginger in its own syrup. Serve with cream. The figs for stewing are the dried ones.

GOOSEBERRIES

Gooseberry Amber

Put 2 oz of butter in a saucepan, add 1 lb of prepared gooseberries and ¼ lb of sugar. Gently heat until the fruit is reduced to a soft, thick mass, then stir in 1 oz of breadcrumbs and 3 egg yolks. Pour the mixture into a buttered dish and bake it for half an hour in a moderate oven, beat up the whites of the eggs to a stiff froth, adding 2 dessertspoons of sugar. Heap this mixture over the gooseberries. Put the dish back and leave it in a cool oven until it is pale golden brown. Serve at once.

Gooseberry Purée

Gooseberry purée made without sugar makes a good sharp sauce to go with grilled or baked mackerel. Simmer the gooseberries with a moistening of water in a covered saucepan with a little butter if desired. When soft push through a sieve.

Gooseberry Pudding

The procedure is the same for gooseberry pudding as for blackberry pudding with twice or more sugar for the gooseberries, depending on the degree of sourness.

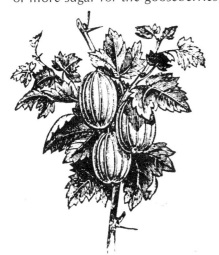

Gooseberry Pie

Lay short pastry over topped, tailed and washed gooseberries, with enough sugar to your taste. Pile the gooseberries high in the dish but add no extra water. Make a hole in the pastry lid to let the steam out, and bake in a medium oven (40 minutes).

Gooseberry Fool

Choose gooseberries that are ripe so that their flavour is well-developed. Levellers is the name given to the largest and best honey-coloured gooseberries. They are sold in the Market. Top and tail and wash them. Put them into a heavy saucepan with about a ¼ inch of water and sugar to taste. Cook them little and gently until they are just soft, then either liquidize them, stems and all, to a rough purée or sieve them. Mix with a nearly equal amount of cream. As an alternative egg custard or a mixture of custard and cream can be used instead of cream alone.

GRAPES

This classic fruit has been the subject of some heavy advertising by the South African Growers. The only ones imported that I especially look forward to are the small seedless white grapes that come very ripe from Cyprus in July and August.

Grapes with Cream and Caramel Crunch

Lay some washed grapes in a dish, peeled if the skins are tough, and cover with at least an inch of stiffly whipped cream. Sprinkle the cream with brown sugar and put under a hot grill for long enough to caramelize the sugar into a toffee topping. The cream and the grapes are not heated up.

GRAPEFRUIT

Grapefruit is at its best in fruit salads, or halved and sweetened if necessary.

GUAVA

This American tropical fruit is grown for the sake of its apple-like flesh. Really ripe, guavas can be eaten as dessert fruit. Guavas are used to make a sweetly delicious jelly. Make this as you would crab-apple jelly, but add some lemon pips in a bag for their pectin and sweeten it to your taste — it takes less sugar than crab-apples.

KUMQUAT

A small bitter-sweet fruit from a shrub of Japanese origin, mainly grown in the southern USA but sometimes seen in greenhouses in England. Cut in halves the fruit may be stewed in a little water until tender, sweetened with some sugar and cooked a little longer to reduce the syrup. When cold serve with vanilla ice.

LEMON

Citron Pudding *(from The London Art of Cookery, 1783)*

"Take a spoonful of fine flour, two ounces of sugar, a little nutmeg, and half a pint of cream. Mix them all well together, with the yolks of three eggs. Put it in to tea-cups, and stick in it two ounces of citron cut up very thin. Bake them in a pretty quick oven, and then turn out upon a China dish."

Syllabub *(from the Robinson family manuscript book of 1840)*

"Take a pint of cream and near as much good white wine, the juice of a lemon and the rind grated fine. Sugar to your taste, mix all together and whisk well. As the froth rises take it off and lay it on a whisk to drain. When you have a sufficient quantity put the remainder in to your glasses and then lay the froth upon it and fill your glasses as high as you like."

Syllabub Under the Cow *(from the London Art of Cookery, 1783)*

"Put into a punch-bowl of cyder and a bottle of strong beer. Grate in a small nutmeg, and sweeten it to your taste. Then milk from the cow as much milk as will make a strong froth. Then let it stand an hour, strew over it a few currants well washed, picked and plumped before the fire, and it will be fit for service."

One hundred years ago there were still cows in Hyde Park much favoured for the making of syllabubs. My grandmother remembered well a woman with a cow she tethered at the foot of the steps into St James Park that are near the Athenaeum Club.

Lemon Syllabub

1 lemon, brandy, 3 oz castor sugar, ½ pint double cream and ½ pint sweet white wine.

Peel the lemon taking off no white pith, squeeze out the juice into a small bowl and together with the rind and enough brandy or sherry to make 1/8 pint. Leave these to marinade overnight. Take out the peel and stir in the sugar until it dissolves. Whip the cream until it just peaks. Gradually add the lemon, brandy and wine beating all the time: the cream should still peak. Pile the mixture into little bowls or glasses and chill overnight. Syllabub will keep for 2 days in a refrigerator.

LIME

This small greenish-yellow fruit, like a miniature lemon, is grown in most sub-tropical countries, chiefly the West Indies. Its juice and rind are used for drinks, in cooking and for preserving in the same way as lemon.

LOGANBERRY

This large, dark raspberry-like fruit was introduced in 1881 by Judge J. H. Logan. It is a hybrid between the American dewberry and the true raspberry. It is good eaten with plenty of sugar and some cream in tarts, pies and jams in the same way as blackberries.

LYCHEE

A Chinese fruit, oval and rarely much more than an inch in diameter. The hard, brown, knobbly skin covers a delicious translucent white flesh, which makes a useful addition to fresh fruit salads or can be eaten plain as a dessert.

MANGO

"The choicest mango has no fibre in the pulp, and for flavour cannot be rivalled by any fruit in the world; but a bad mango tastes like a tow soaked in oil of turpentine. Mangoes should not be eaten freshly plucked from the tree, but gathered when ripe and laid upon a shelf for a few days until mature."

Neil Leitch, *Dietetics in Warm Climates,* London 1930.

With the stone taken out, mangoes can be put into curries; made into a pickle with salt, oil and chilli peppers, or made into a preserve by boiling in syrup. The flesh can be mixed with cream to a fool, or the juice may be squeezed out and the flesh dried on plates making little Indian cakes called Ambsath. Salted mangoes are eaten in Africa with fish curries.

MEDLAR

When it looks unattractive — like a rotten crab-apple — it is soft and ready to eat. The taste is thought to go well with port as a dessert, but medlars, like guavas, are really best made into a jelly.

MELON

Melons like marrows, cucumbers, pumpkins — all members of the gourd family — come to the Market in several varieties. The most important are the cantaloup, honeydew, scarlet flesh, tiger and, of course, the water melon. Best eaten alone, slightly chilled, if really ripe; otherwise they may require a little sugar and powdered ginger.

Melon Patricia

I asked Richard Buckle to contribute a recipe. Ballet critic for the *Sunday Times*, distinguished writer on art and theatre, he has lived since the beginning of the 1960s close to the Royal Opera House and overlooking the market. Melons are particularly seductive if you walk around Covent Garden when they are at their ripest:

"Scalp an Ogee melon and remove the pips. Scoop out the flesh and mix it in a bowl with shrimps and curry powder. Spoon the mixture into the melon, replace the scalp, and put it in the refrigerator.

"Because the melon comes from Israel, the frozen shrimps from Iceland and the curry powder from India, I always serve this first course on blue and white soup plates from Hong Kong; and I call it after the darling woman who taught it to me, who is Australian."

NECTARINE

A smooth-skinned variety of peach, small, firmer and with a richer flavour. Nectarines are really too good to be cooked but they can be prepared as peaches.

ORANGES

Orange Marmalade

The best, bitter-tasting marmalade is made with Seville oranges that are only available for a few weeks after Christmas.

Cut 2 lbs of oranges into halves, remove the pips, saving any juice and slice finely. Put it all in a saucepan with 2½ pints of water and simmer slowly until the peel is soft. Add 3 lbs of sugar, pre-warmed in a tray in the oven. The marmalade should then be boiled rapidly to reduce it to exactly 5 lbs in weight or until the mixture sets when a drop is left to cool on a saucer. Take off the heat when the setting point is reached and after 10 minutes it is ready to be put into pots.

Orange Surprise

Robert Bruce-Steel, a fruit merchant at the most north-westerly corner of the central Market, can recall the flower Market when women were porters and some of the older women sat along the northern edge of the central Market shelling peas into their aprons as fast as their fingers would move, which could equal the speed of a modern machine. He started work at Covent Garden Market in 1925. He has given the following dessert to friends and it was always well received.

"From a large orange slice the top and after incising with a sharp knife scoop out the flesh, saving any good segments for final decoration. Pour a little liqueur over the flesh of the orange and mix, together with sugar if desired, the pulp with some vanilla ice-cream. Pack it back into the orange, top with whipped cream and decorate with a few orange segments. Chill until required."

Oranges in Syrup *(from Mr Gonzales)*

Peel whole oranges and take off all the pith. Cut some of the skin into tiny thin strips (julienne) and boil these for a few minutes in water to take away any bitterness.

Put a mixture of half sugar, half lemon juice into a saucepan and heat it gently until the sugar melts and you have a syrup. Put the syrup aside to cool.

To serve, open out the orange into segments to make a flower shape, remove any pith from the centre and lay some strips of peel on them and pour the syrup over.

PAPAYA OR PAWPAW

Large gourd-like fruits with thick rinds that can be eaten like melon with sugar, ginger or a squeeze of fresh lime. When it is still green the fruit is peeled, boiled, and cut into small pieces and served with an oil and vinegar or lemon dressing. Its juice has the interesting property of tenderizing meat.

PASSION FRUIT OR GRENADILLA

Use a teaspoon to scoop out the moist pippy pulp. This is improved by adding a little sherry or cream and sugar to your taste. It makes a good juice for fruit cups, or to add to gin.

Passion Fruit Curd

Mix the pulp of 6 passion fruits with ½ lb of sugar and the juice of 2 lemons; lightly beat 2 eggs and put all the ingredients in a double-boiler over a moderate heat. Stir occasionally, and when the mixture thickens cook for 15 minutes longer, stirring frequently.

PEACHES

Peaches in Wine

Peel the peaches, slice them, sprinkle with sugar and a little lemon juice, cover with wine and chill.

Peach Melba

Named in honour of Dame Nellie Melba. Ripe peaches are peeled and halved, then laid on vanilla ice cream and covered with fresh raspberry purée.

PEARS

The two main varieties that are sold are the Conference, the long, rather green ones which are not only eaten as dessert, but can also be cooked or bottled, and the Comice, which melts in the mouth.

Early on some very small pears are sold that are very woody and unpromising but they can be stewed whole, unpeeled in cider, with a clove or two and some honey and are a great delicacy with me. Cook them very slowly and give them enough time to soften (1 hour). The syrup can be thickened either by separating from the pears and reducing it by boiling or by thickening it with a little cornflour, making sure to cook the cornflour long enough to lose the floury taste. They are good hot or cold.

Sliced Pear with Sherry

Peel and slice ripe Conference pears, leave just covered in sherry for one hour in the refrigerator. Serve with brown sugar and cream.

Pears Belle Hélène

Poach peeled ripe pears with sugar, water and vanilla. Allow to cool. Serve on vanilla ice-cream with chocolate sauce.

Pear Condé

Serve the same poached pears on dollops of rice pudding. Pour a little apricot jam moistened with kirsch over the pears before serving.

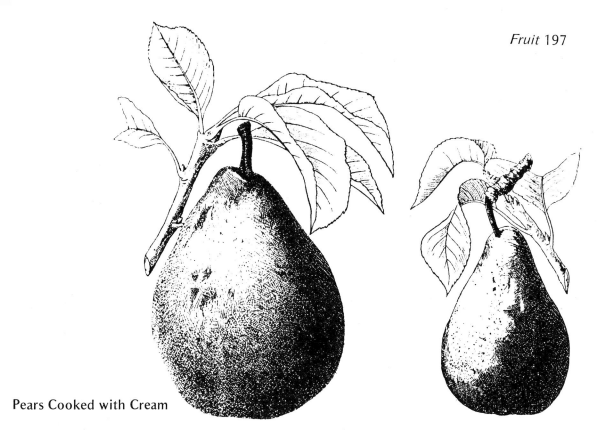

Pears Cooked with Cream

Peel 2 lbs of not quite ripe dessert pears, cut them in ½ inch slices and cut out the cores and pips. Put them in one layer on a well buttered flame-proof dish. Sprinkle over 4 heaped tablespoons of white sugar and ½ teaspoon of vanilla extract. Simmer very gently until the pears are tender (10-20 minutes). Pour over the pears ¼ pint of double cream. Shake the pan over the heat until the cream thickens which only takes a minute or two. Sprinkle with brown sugar and serve, or if the oven is hot put the dish in for a few minutes until a golden skin forms over the cream.

Pears Stewed in Red Wine *(from Mr Gonzales)*

This is a good way of dealing with rock-hard pears.

Peel 2 lbs of pears and stand them in an oven proof dish; sprinkle 3 oz white sugar over them and pour over ½ pint of red wine; then cover with water. Bake in a very slow oven for 5-7 hours, basting them with the wine occasionally, until the pears are soft and turned brown. Leave to cool and serve together with the juice on a white plate. They go well with cold creamed rice or thick cream.

PERSIMMON

Called a kaki in France and Italy, it has to look horrible, a little old and squashed, and then it is ready and delicious to eat. Cut them in half and eat the flesh with a spoon, or mix the flesh with cream to a fool.

PINEAPPLES

Pineapple with Kirsch

Cut slices of pineapple, about ½ an inch thick, and cut off the skin. Lay the slices flat on a dish and sprinkle with kirsch and a little sugar. Leave in the refrigerator for 10 minutes before serving.

Ananas Creole

Scoop or cut the flesh from a medium sized pineapple. Skin 3 bananas and 3 oranges; slice the bananas into rings and mash the oranges, taking out any pips or pith. Mix with the pineapple. Take a little grated coconut and mix with the other fruit, add sugar to taste and the juice of one lemon. Refill the pineapple shell and chill it for some time before serving.

Pineapple Fritters

A fresh pineapple can disappoint by being neither sufficiently juicy nor with the full scent or flavour. Then try dipping ½ inch slices in batter and deep frying. Give them sufficient time in the oil to heat right through (5 minutes).

    The crisp batter by contrast makes the pineapple taste the better. Serve immediately with a sprinkle of castor sugar.

Pineapple auction, 1912

PHYSALIS

Can be eaten as sweets boiled in syrup, covered in marzipan but are probably best made into jam.

PLUMS

Most of the plums eaten are varieties of the *Prunus domestica,* of Asiatic origin, although there is an American species, *Prunus americana,* which has a lot of cultivated varieties.

Greengages are rated the best dessert plums to be eaten fresh and ripe. Sharper tasting plums cook better and damsons are very good for pies, crumbles and for making jams and jellies.

The plum, apart from denoting a good thing in life, is also a somewhat obsolete word for a raisin, hence plum pudding, plum duff, plum cake and so forth.

Baked Plums

Large plums, washed and stoned, are piled in a pyramid on a baking dish, sprinkled with sugar and moistened with a tablespoon of water. Bake in a low oven until soft but stop before they lose their shape (45 minutes).

Serve hot with shortbread.

Plum Compôte

Make a syrup by boiling half a cup of sugar with each cup of water. Drop the plums into the boiling syrup then simmer until just softening. Remove the plums and boil away the syrup until it is the desired consistency and can be poured back over the plums. This correct and classic method uses a lot of sugar, though, if you find this undesirable on health grounds or because you do not like such a sweet taste, you can thicken the syrup with cornflour instead. Serve cold with cream or with hot custard.

Plum Pie

The plums settle on cooking, so the pie dish should be completely full of fruit. Add a moistening of water and sprinkle with sugar before covering with short pastry.

Plums in a Pudding

Plums make a good pudding in suet used in the same way as blackberries.

Plum Sponge

Put a single layer of plums in a baking dish that is about three inches deep and just cover the fruit with sponge mix. Bake in a hot oven until golden in colour, and a knife inserted comes out clean (30 minutes).

Damson Purée

Gently cook a pound of damsons with a tablespoonful of water until they disintegrate. Pass through a sieve to remove stems and stones. Sweeten to taste by dissolving sugar in the purée.

It is good served chilled with cream or egg custard.

Damson Mousse

Make a purée and before cooling melt into it one ounce of gelatine per pint. Allow to cool until it begins to set then whisk it. Fold in two stiffly beaten egg whites and stand in a cool place to set.

Serve with cream.

Damson Pudding

Damsons make a good pudding. Prepare in the same way as blackberry pudding, adding twice the amount of sugar.

Damson Pie

Put a pound of damsons in a pie dish with 2 oz of sugar and a tablespoon of water. Cover with shortcrust pastry, sprinkle with sugar and bake in a slow oven (1 hour).

Damson Fool

Damson fool is particularly good because of the sharp taste of the damsons and the marvellous colour. Mix well equal quantities of damson purée with cream. Prepare when the purée is cool and serve cold.

PRICKLY PEAR

This cactus grows readily in many warm countries — too readily for Australia and parts of Africa where its introduction has created a weed of menacing proportions. Pleasant tasting, it is only worth bothering with if strict precautions are taken to avoid the frightening spines, the smallest ones being the most troublesome; it should only be handled on the end of a fork. First chill the fruit and, using a fork to hold it, score the skin as with an orange in order to peel it off in segments which should include all the prickles. The white flesh inside is eaten fresh.

QUINCE

The quince was the "golden apple" of the ancients, an emblem of love and happiness: Chaucer mentions it growing in England. It is either pear-shaped or round with a yellow woolly skin and yellow flesh which turns pink in cooking. It makes excellent jams and jellies and was once added to English apple pies.

RASPBERRIES

Raspberries, with strawberries, are the most popular of all small dessert fruit. They are best served with a little sugar and cream or in any way suitable for strawberries. They also make excellent jam and jelly.

Raspberry Vinegar *(from Marcel Boulestin)*

"Fill a jar with ripe raspberries, press them very lightly and add as much vinegar as the jar will take. After one month, strain the liquid. A teaspoonful in a glass of cold sugared water makes a delicious beverage."

RED CURRANTS,

WHITE CURRANTS

These cultivated hybrids of at least three wild berries are used in jams, pies and summer puddings. Redcurrant jelly, as well as being a jam, accompanies lamb, mutton, venison and hare, and is used in the making of Cumberland and Oxford sauces.

Red Currant Jelly (1837)

"Pick the currants, put them into a jar. Set them on a fire in a pan with water. Steam about ½ an hour, or until the juice is extracted, then run it through a cotton bag or fine hair sieve. This should be done in the evening before you make the jelly. To every pint of juice put 1 lb of single refined sugar. Set the juice with the sugar on the fire and take care to skim carefully as it comes to the boil. Let it boil for 8 minutes, which should be sufficient. Put into small jars and put these in an extremely cool but not damp place. This jelly will keep for years."

A mixture of red and white currants will also make a good jelly.

RHUBARB

The first of the home-grown "fruits" in the new year, with the best main crop coming to the market in the spring.

To cook rhubarb cut the stalks into short lengths and put into a pan with just enough water to prevent the rhubarb burning, plenty of sugar, a good knob of butter and a little lemon peel. Cover and cook over a low heat until tender (10 minutes).

Rhubarb Fool

Allow cooked rhubarb to cool, then stir in as much cream as you care to use. Chill and serve.

Rhubarb Pie

Butter an oven-proof dish and fill it with chopped rhubarb. Pour in a little water, plenty of sugar, then dot with lemon peel and butter before covering with short crust pastry. Bake in a medium oven (40 minutes).

Rhubarb Crumble

Prepare the rhubarb as for a pie but with half the amount of sugar. Top with crumble mixture.

Rhubarb Snow

Beat the whites of two eggs until stiff. Fold half the beaten egg white into some cooked rhubarb and put the mixture into a deep dish. Pile the remaining egg white on top. Lightly brown in a hot oven (10 minutes).

SLOE

In England a sloe is the fruit of the Blackthorn, and it makes one of the oldest liqueurs, Sloe Gin. In the USA the name is given to various acid plums. To make jams and jellies, mix sloes with apples.

Sloe and Apple Cake

2½ lb apples, 1½ lb of sloes and ½ lb sugar to each 1 lb of pulp.

Gently cook the apples and sloes with minimum amount of water; when they are tender strain off the juice and pulp and mix this with ½ lb of sugar to every pound of fruit pulp. Boil the mixture until it sets (30-45 minutes).
   Pour it into dessert bowls to set and serve with cream or custard.

STRAWBERRIES

This fruit floods into Covent Garden during its brief summer season, always raising expectations for everyone along the line: growers, wholesalers, greengrocers, shoppers and their families. The price in the Market rattles up and down so vigorously, mainly according to the weather, that the growers and wholesalers must come to regard the whole business as a rather frantic nightmare. The fruit themselves, however, usually live up to expectations.

Everyone must have their favourite way of eating soft fruit but it is worth listing a few of the many suggestions, mentioning perhaps as a preface that strawberries must be washed before eating. With lemon juice alone; with their points dipped in salt; with castor sugar and claret or champagne poured over them; mashed with sugar and fresh cream; with chopped bananas; with chopped fresh pineapple; made into mousse with cream.

The most expensive strawberries to be found in the Market are the small alpine ones. If you get them really ripe try them by the first method — plain with lemon juice.

UGLI

Tangelo is a prettier, American name for the ugli (or ugly) which looks like a giant dirty-yellow tangerine with pinkish grapefruit-like segments inside. The flesh is easily separated from pith and skin and breaks up into small pieces that are a good addition to a fresh fruit salad.

ALGINATE HOUSE AND DEEP FROZEN MOUSSE

Alginate House, with its distinctive stone carving, dominates the northern corner of Henrietta and Bedford Street. This beautiful building, originally professional apartments, was completed in 1857, when the architect, Charles Gray, was about 28. At 18 he had been co-founder of the Architectural Association and was a leading designer of the 1850s. Alginates are extracts from certain types of seaweed. One of their many uses is in the manufacturing of foods and drinks. Sodium alginate stabilizes the foam on beer, prevents separation in emulsions such as mayonnaise and ice-cream and allows more air and water content to be included in cakes, pies, jams and so on. The following recipe is from the Alginates Food Recipe Book:

Manucol DM is used as the gelling agent and stabiliser in deep frozen mousse which can be prepared in standard ice cream making equipment. The product has a pleasant eating texture on thawing and is free from syneresis.

Examples:

	i(neutral) (Parts by weight)	ii(acidic) (Parts by weight)
Manucol DM	10	10
Sugar	175	175
Dextrose	100	100
Skimmed milk powder	80	—
Vegetable fat	150	150
Glyceryl mono-stearate	5	5
Disodium phosphate	2.0	3.5
Water	1000	1000
Citric acid	—	4
Dicalcium phosphate anhydrous	—	2.5

Note: If the ice cream machine does not include air injection facilities, it is recommended that 8 to 10 parts by weight of a whipping agent are included in an admixture with other dry ingredients (see 2 below).

Method of Use:

1. Mix the Manucol DM with 10 times its weight of sugar and the disodium phosphate and dissolve in water.
2. Heat the Manucol DM solution to 50°C and add the skimmed milk powder (or citric acid and dicalcium phosphate anhydrous) with the glyceryl mono-stearate followed by addition of the sugar and dextrose (and whipping agent if required).
3. Melt the fat and add to the mix at 70°C with good stirring. Pasteurise at 70°C-75°C.

4. *Homogenise at approximately 140Kg/sq.cm (2000psi).*
5. *Cool to 30^oC and pass into a holding tank equipped with a slow speed stirrer.*
6. *Freeze at -2^oC to -5^oC and an overrun of 100%.*
7. *Discharge in container and chill to -20^oC. Store and distribute in deep freeze conditions.*

The coffee stall under the portico of St Paul's, 1974

A WALK FROM THE STRAND TO ST MARTIN'S LANE THROUGH COVENT GARDEN, 1974

The Adelphi Theatre, half-way along the Strand on the north side. A day in June; windy not summery. Followed the paper bags blowing westerly along the Strand. Cut up Bull Inn Court, tiled and ale-stained. Two tramps sleeping in cardboard boxes among the abandoned rubbish in a disused doorway to the Adelphi gallery. Detour left into Maiden Lane to examine yellow-painted Royal Arms over the Monarch's Entrance. Turn westwards, leaving on the right Rules Restaurant, Recherché Table d'Hôte, *Luncheons, Dinners and Late Suppers: the brass plate burnished until the letters fade. The mullioned windows with stained-glass of Sussex mansions squint at Corpus Christi Roman Catholic Church.*

Northwards, up Southampton Street, the nets of cabbages piled against the Tuscan columns. Samuel French's theatre bookshop, the very plain door concealing Boulestin's famous restaurant. R.W. Mitchell sells beetroots from Kent and apples and pears, but the cherries come later. Outside, on the pavement, tightly-packed Dorchester watercress; from Woking comes tarragon, bay leaves in bundles, mustard and cress. Jas. Butler has written his sign on the wall: Herbalist, Seedsman, Lavender Water etc. Back under the cover is the haggler's corner, Neirotti and Page keeps the Chinese provisioned.

Facing St Paul's, with the Market behind, salads are sold: lettuces, radishes. Under the church portico a dozen persons of no fixed address surround a fire, never wandering far from the coffee stall. A hundred pigeons have the same idea. A tablet in the wall commemorates the first Punch and Judy as seen by Pepys. Walk to the corner of King Street; Lord Archer's 1718 house, opposite, is now George Monroe Produce Ltd, piled with foreign produce from the south Mediterranean: Valencia late oranges, grade 1, TBZ treated, in diphenyl, waxed, from Cyprus. Crated fruit on barrows is pushed briskly down King Street, past the Essex Serpent, where once a snake took refuge after stealing a ride in a crate from Essex. No refuge or drink for the traveller out of hours; market men only allowed.

Turn down the passage into churchyard where Mr Hatch the verger encourages flowers, discourages dogs and children. Up the steps, into the church, take a leaflet and read all about it: the actors' church, destroyed by fire, reconstructed, barn-like, but "the handsomest barn in England". Straight down the garden through Inigo Place into Bedford Street. Walk up towards Moss Bros, the narrow street, left, is New Row, but the main road is taken to the corner of Rose Street. Turn right. Flanked by commercial solidity, the 1860 Auction Rooms, waiting empty for degutting. Up Rose Street towards the Lamb and Flag, through Lazenby Court where Dryden suffered cowardly assault and into Floral Street. Turn left, back towards Garrick Street, where the old glass works, like a renovated monastery, has become the Inigo Jones, a stylish restaurant. Peer into Club opposite, through grand mahogany door which frames The Garrick's collection of theatrical portraits. Ahead, at the lights, is St Martin's Lane.

The colonnade on the north side of the Piazza, showing the door of Lord Archer's house, 1974

FLOWERS FOR EATING

Flower market, 1873

BROOM BUDS

The almond-flavoured buds of the yellow broom were used as capers.

CAPERS

Capers are the flower-buds of the caper bush. They are preserved in vinegar.

CARNATIONS

Carnation recipes are often found in 17th-and 18th-century books and manuscripts: ratafias, which are fruits and flowers pressed and mixed with brandy, syrup and spices and kept for a month or so before straining and bottling, also carnation butters, cordials, syrups and vinegars. The petals, chopped, can be added to biscuits and cakes or put in salads.

Carnation Fondants

Grind to a pulp about half a cup of red carnation petals. Gradually add to it the white of one egg, icing sugar and a pinch of powdered clove. Continue adding the sugar until you have a smooth stiff paste. Make rosettes through an icing tube or flatten it out and make tiny squares or circles. Allow to dry. These quantities will make between 24-30 sweets.

CHRYSANTHEMUMS

All chrysanthemums have the same strong smell and taste of autumn. First choose your colour and then float the petals on a steaming tureen of broth. The petals can also go into salads.

COWSLIP SYRUP

Take 12 oz of fresh cowslip flowers and one pint of boiling water. Infuse twenty-four hours, strain, and then add 2 lb of white sugar. Boil it gently until it attains the consistency of a syrup.

DANDELION SALAD

Wash and dry half a cup of dandelion buds. Cut two rashers of smoked bacon into strips and fry until the fat runs. Toss in the dandelion buds and cook until the buds burst open. Empty the frying pan, fat and all, onto some tender dandelion leaves and sprinkle a little vinegar, lemon juice or vinaigrette on the salad.

MARIGOLDS

The marigold's bright petals have long been used as a herb and as a colourant. Fresh or dried it is good in puddings, cakes, salads and meat dishes, it colours rice, noodles and soups.

To dry the petals spread them on a baking tray or foil and cook in a very slow oven for two hours or until they are dry enough to crumble. Store them in airtight jars ready for use.

Eggs to look like Marigolds

Hard boil your eggs, peel and slice them in half lengthways. Take out the yolks and mash them together with some mayonnaise, dried and crushed marigold petals and a little pepper. Refill the egg whites with this mixture. Take fresh marigold petals and tuck them into the centres of the stuffed eggs until each egg is a flower.

MARROW FLOWERS

These flowers in Italy are sold in the markets. Stuffed with rice and herbs and cooked in oil they are served cold. Try dipping them in batter and deep frying.

NASTURTIUM SALAD

Nasturtium is rich in vitamin C.

Arrange some of the leaves around the bowl and shred more with lettuce, heaping these in the centre. Decorate with nasturtium flowers. Serve the dressing, preferably a light creamy one — it could be watered down mayonnaise — in a separate jug.

Flower market, 1973

PRIMROSE

Primrose leaves, when young, can be eaten boiled like sorrel, preferably with sorrel or lettuce as they do not have a strong taste. Primrose flowers look fresh and pretty in salads or floating on almond or chicken broth.

ROSES

The sweetest smelling roses are the best to eat. The older simpler varieties such as cabbage, damask, Moss, Rugosa have more fragrance and a more delicate texture.

"Crystallized" Rose Petals

These are lovely as decoration for cakes and puddings or served as sweets.

Slightly beat the white of one egg, a little cochineal added gives a good colour. Choose the sweetest smelling fresh red or pink rose petals, dip each petal first into the egg and then into white granulated sugar, be sure to coat all surfaces completely. Put the petals on an ungreased baking tray and dry them in the sun or in a very slow oven until firm and crystallized. To store put them between grease proof paper in an airtight tin. Whole Violet flowers can be crystallized in the same way.

Rose Butter

Spread about 3 cupfuls of rose petals on ungreased baking trays and dry them on a slow oven. When thoroughly dry, place in a deep casserole in layers, sprinkling each layer liberally with salt. Place butter on top. Cover the casserole tightly and leave the butter there for two or three days. It will absorb the rose petal fragrance and flavour. Use for making plain little cakes and biscuits or for spreading on buns, toast or bread for tea.

Rose Diaboliche *(Diabolical Roses)*

"2 eggs, 3 oz of flour, the juice of half a lemon, a tablespoonful of olive oil. Mix the ingredients into a batter. Throw into mix some velvety red roses, with the outside petals cut away and just a couple of inches of stalk left, and fry them in boiling oil."

From *La Cucina Futurista* by Marinetti published in 1932. Perhaps the most amazing of all cookery books full of exotic inventions, many of them very good — try pineapple with sardines or mortadella wrapped around plain nougat! This rose recipe is recommended for brides to eat at midnight in January.

Lozenges of Red Roses *(17th century)*

"Boil your sugar to sugar again (i.e. till it candies), then put in your red roses, being finely beaten, and made moist with the juice of a lemon. Let it not boil after the roses are in, but pour it upon a pie plate and cut it into what form you please."

Oil of Roses *(from a cooks' manuscript book written in the year of Waterloo, 1815*

"This is a very nice liqueur. To one quart of brandy add one pound of roses with the best scent; add one third of a pint of water, let them infuse for a week in a jar, and then distil. After distilling, add a syrup of ½ lb of sugar dissolved in one pint of water, and a little filtered cochineal for colouring."

The last flower girl

Rose Petal Jam *(traditional recipe from Surrey)*

"Make a syrup of one pound of loaf sugar and as little rose-water as you can do with. Take a pound of rose petals (cabbage rose with the strongest scent are best) and dry them in a shady place. Scald them for a moment in boiling water, then drain and dry them, and add them with a spoonful of orange-flower water to the syrup. Boil in a preserving-pan until the jam will 'set' or 'jell' when dropped upon a plate. When it has cooled off a little, pour it into pots, and cover up well, the usual way."

> "Conserve of Roses comforteth the stomach, the heart and all the bowels, it mollifieth and softeneth, and it is good against black cholera and melancholy. Conserve of White Roses is more laxative than the red."
>
> *The Treasure of Hidden Secrets,* 1637, compiled by John Partride.

Rose Water *(1783 manuscript)*

"Gather your red roses when they be dry and full blown; pick off the leaves, and to every peck (2 gallons) put a quart of water. Then put them into a cold still and make a slow fire under it; for the slower you distil it, the better it will be. Then bottle it, and in two or three days time you may cork it."

This recipe is also good for orange flower water.

(1 pint rose petals to 1/8 pint water, i.e. about half a wine glass.)

Right and far right: statuary on the roof of the market building

SUNFLOWERS

"Ere it comes to expand and show its golden face (the sunflower) being dress'd as the artichouk, is eaten as a daintie."   John Evelyn, 1699.

"The buds before they be flowered, boyled and eaten with butter, vinegar and pepper, are exceeding pleasant meat or they may be broiled upon a gridiron and eaten with oil and vinegar."   Gerards *Herball*, 1633.

OIL OF VIOLETS

Boil three ounces of dried violets for two minutes with water and sugar, strain and filter, and add to spirits and syrup.

Above: the market during the first world war

Right, top and bottom: the market in 1912

THE TURN OF THE CENTURY

The Duke of Bedford was already interested in selling the Market area as early as 1882 but the local authorities he approached turned it down. The Duke persisted and offered it for private sale. The taunts in the press and the complaints from the public and traders about the conditions in the market and the high tolls contributed a lot to his determination to get rid of it.

Eventually, the sale was arranged with Sir Joseph Beecham but he died in 1918 and the sale contract was completed by the Covent Garden Estate Company. Sir Joseph had paid 2½ million pounds for it. Covent Garden Properties, later Covent Garden Market Ltd, took over the property in 1924.

The Market had its first brief strike in 1891. There were further strikes in 1911 and 1924. The pitchers, porters and warehousemen failed on these occasions to achieve their demands. In 1936 the Transport and General Workers Union formed a Covent Garden Branch at the time of a further wage dispute. Now the workers were able to unite and strike together and agreement with the employers was negotiated.

After the war big changes in the market had to wait until 1957 when the three groups – porters, pitchers and warehousemen – were all brought into one category and known as porters. The Runciman Committee reported in the same year, and by 1961 a Bill was passed which set up the Covent Garden Market Authority and acquired the property. The Authority, appointed by the Minister of Agriculture, was charged with providing "better market facilities for the trade, to concentrate market activities into a more compact area and eventually to rebuild the market, either on the present site or on a new one, within the Covent Garden area".

NUTS

ALMONDS

There are two types of almonds; the sweet and the bitter. Although the bitter have a better taste they yield poisonous prussic acid when crushed, so it is advisable to use them in moderation. Sweet almonds are eaten, salted or not, before, or after dinner with port. They come to the Market from August to Christmas and Jordan almonds are thought to be the best.

Almond Milk

Blanch, peel and chop two dozen almonds, put them into a jug with a pint of water. Stir this well until it clouds like milk. Strain out the almonds. Pound them to a pulp and stir them in the water again. Add sugar and a little orange juice to taste. Served chilled, this makes a good summer drink.

Almond Tart *(from Marcel Boulestin)*

Make a short pastry and line a tart tin with it. For the filling mix together 2 eggs, 3 oz sugar, 3 oz of pounded or ground almonds and a wine glass of milk. Bake in a fairly hot oven for 15 minutes. Sprinkle sugar on top 2 or 3 minutes before it is ready and serve it hot or cold with cream.

Burnt Almonds, White *(from an 1815 manuscript)*

"Take some of the finest Jordan Almonds you can get, and sift all the dust from them; then have some syrup boiling in a pan, let it boil till it comes almost to a caramel; put your almonds in, and stir them till they are cold; put them in your sieve, break those that stick together, and then have another pan of syrup boiling, the same as before, and give them two coats of sugar; when done, pick them from each other."

Burnt almonds are called pralines in France. To make them pink or red add cochineal to a syrup, more in the last than the first.

Almond Fritters

2 oz ground almonds, ½ oz cornflour, 2 eggs, 1 oz castor sugar and a few drops of vanilla.

Mix the egg yolks, cornflour, ground almonds and vanilla together. Beat the egg whites stiffly and add them to the mixture. Fry drops of the mixture in hot fat, drain, cover in sugar and serve them hot.

CHESTNUTS

A very seasonable item in the Market, appearing only round about Christmas, sweet chestnuts seem better when bought than gathered wild from the English countryside, since the older you are the smaller the ones from the woods seem to get. The name is said to come from a Greek place name, and describes not only the Spanish or sweet chestnut, but also the inedible horse chestnut. A chestnut is also a stale anecdote, presumably because of their very brief shelf life, a further consequence of which is that they sometimes appear out of season, from cans, as chestnut purée. Although the sweetened purée is quite good, tasting like the much more expensive marrons glacés that have been ground up, the unsweetened never seems much use as a substitute for the real thing, as it may have a rather gluey consistency and lacks enough of the right taste.

To shell chestnuts, score each across the rounded side and put into boiling water for long enough (8-10 minutes) to make the shell break off when squeezed then remove the skin with a sharp knife. Cook by simmering in salted water until soft.

Chestnut Purée

Prepare the chestnuts by scoring, boiling for 10 minutes, shelling and skinning and then simmer in a mixture of ½ milk and ½ stock or water until they are soft (1 hour) and the liquid has nearly all evaporated away. Use a liquidizer to make the purée or push them through a sieve. If the mixture turns too dry, mix butter into it. Before serving with game or meat, stir some of the juice into the purée.

Devilled Chestnuts

This dish is good with game, ham, rabbit and hare. Boil shelled and skinned chestnuts gently in water till they are tender. Drain them, be careful not to break them, sprinkle with salt and a little cayenne pepper and fry them in oil for two minutes.

COCONUT ICE *(from a 19th-century Hampshire manuscript)*

"Take one grated fresh coconut, two pounds of loaf sugar, a small piece of butter, one tablespoon of cream, a little cochineal. (A very large nut will require three pounds of sugar, and water in proportion.) Take the coconut milk, and add water sufficient to make half a pint all together. Add the sugar, and boil well together for ten minutes, then stir in the grated nut and boil another ten minutes. Take off the fire, add the cream, beat the mixture well until it begins to set. Pour half into a buttered soup-plate; add a little cochineal to the other half, and pour this on top of the first when it sets enough to bear it. When cold, cut it up into strips."

FILBERTS

These nuts grow in every part of the British Isles but in Kent they are commercially grown. The Kentish Cob is a type of filbert. The name is a corruption of "Nuts of St Philibert" whose feast day happens to be August 22, when the filberts are usually ready to be picked.

Candied Filberts *(traditional recipe)*

"Blanch them, and when the skins are removed, let them simmer in very thin syrup for about an hour: put them to cool, and then set them on to the fire again, adding more sugar, until the syrup has become so thick as to candy when cold: take out the filberts before the syrup is cold, and cover them well with pounded loaf sugar: then dry in the sun or in a slow oven. The syrup may be used for any other preserve."

HAZELNUT

This is a type of filbert. Although hazelnuts grow in England they are not commercially cultivated here. In the market, cobs or filberts are the home-grown nuts and the hazels are imported.

PECAN

One of the hickory family of the southern USA this nut is oblong in shape with a thin reddish shell.

Georgia Pecan Brownies

2 egg whites, ¼ lb of chopped pecans, ¼ lb brown sugar, ¼ lb breadcrumbs and 1 teaspoon maple syrup.

Beat the egg whites stiff and add the sugar and syrup to them. Mix the nuts and breadcrumbs and fold in the whites. Make small balls of the mixture and put them on a greased baking tray to cook in a slow oven until brown.

PISTACHIO

This oblong greenish nut has a good flavour, a beautiful pale green colour and makes a lovely icecream. Marinetti, in his book *The Futurist Kitchen,* recommends stuffing dates with chopped pistachio to serve with pork chops in lemon and garlic sauce.

WALNUTS

Known as English walnuts in the USA. In England they rarely ripen and are usually pickled. The walnuts in the Market in time for Christmas come from France.

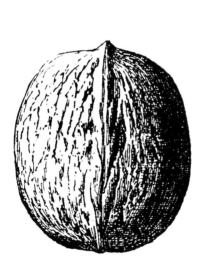 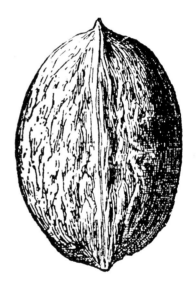

Walnut Bars

2 oz butter, 2 oz lard, ¼ cup boiling water, ¼ lb brown sugar, 2 tablespoons molasses, 10 oz self-raising flour, ½ tablespoon ginger, $\frac{1}{3}$ teaspoon grated nutmeg, teaspoon grated clove, chopped walnuts and 1 teaspoon salt.

Pour the boiling water over the butter and lard and stir in sugar, molasses, flour, salt and spices. When it is thick and evenly mixed leave it to chill. Roll it out and cut it into little bar shapes. Cover these with walnuts and bake in a moderate oven for just ten minutes.

Nut Loaf

¾ lb spinach or other light greens, 1 onion, handful chopped parsley, 3 tablespoons oil, 1 clove of garlic, 1 teaspoon oregano or marjoram, ground walnuts, almonds or pecans, or a combination, 3 oz breadcrumbs, 2 oz wheatgerm, 6 tablespoons tomato sauce and 1 tablespoon soy sauce.

Chop and steam the greens for 5 minutes, chop and saute the onion, parsley, garlic and oregano. Mix the breadcrumbs, wheat germ, tomato and soy sauce and nuts together and add the vegetables to them. Shape into a loaf and bake in a moderate oven for 30 minutes.

The walnut harvest, 1909

TEAS FROM THE GARDEN

Try lime blossom, hollyhock, violet, rose, borage flowers, orange flowers, marigold flowers. Flowers should be pulled from any green parts, left to dry in a shady place and when they are quite dry put into paper bags or tins and kept in a dark place. Delicate flavours are lost easily, so make sure that the water is fresh tasting and that the infusion is made in a clean jug.

"For the Sciatica: decoction of asparagus roots drunk" — Leonard Sowerby, The Ladies Dispensatory, *1652.*

BLACKBERRY leaves — for coughs.

"CABBAGE water drunk is good for colds, catarrh and bronchitis" — Leonard Sowerby, ibid.

CAMOMILE — soothes insomniacs' nerves but never use an odd number of heads for the infusion.

CELERY — for rheumatics, 1 oz of seeds per pint.

DANDELION — for liver and pure blood.

ELDER flowers — brings out fevers and helps colds.

FENNEL — for trouble in the head, just use the leaves.

LETTUCE — a soporific to induce drowsiness.

PARSLEY — for liver trouble, use the root.

ROSEMARY — a gastric stimulant and soothing for people suffering from chest trouble. Use leaves and flowers.

SAGE — settles nerves, relieves bronchitis.

Tramps under the portico of St Paul's **Right: glass roof of the market, 1974**

A SELECTIVE DIARY OF RECENT EVENTS

1961   Parliamentary Bill passed setting up Covent Garden Market Authority charged with rebuilding the Market within the Covent Garden area.

1964   The Authority decides to move Market to Nine Elms, Battersea. Traffic congestion is reason given for this change of mind.

1966-8   Gestation and publication of draft plan for the development of the Covent Garden area after the Market has moved.

1968 onwards   Gentrification of the area as the original local shops start to be taken over by smart restaurants, photographic studios, architects' offices, craft shops and so on.

1970   Publication of the Greater London Council's Covent Garden Joint Development Committee's Revised Plan for the Proposed Comprehensive Development Area.

Spring 1970   Formation of Covent Garden Community Association at a public meeting. The Association opposes GLC plan.

1971-3   Diverse activity by Community Association and other opposition groups. However, a survey shows 800 residents out of 3,500 leaving the area.

1973   Geoffrey Rippon, Secretary of State for the Environment, asks GLC to modify plan. He includes the listing of 250 buildings of historic or architectural interest. The GLC plan cannot survive this and is abandoned. Beaten by the protest movement, the GLC joins it by proposing a locally elected Forum with a consultative role.

1974   GLC reaches decision on disposition of car parking meters for after the Market is moved in October. This is the only firm proposal the Council has currently in hand for the future of the area.

Demolition of the Odhams building in Long Acre

The irony of Covent Garden: the Market goes, but the buildings and sites remain empty.
The land, at market values, is too expensive for any socially acceptable use.

THE OCCUPATION JOB

"Right at the beginning there were two people who were the spokesmen for the movement in the public eye and in the papers. They were myself and Ned. He was a student. We were the leaders. In the end we quarrelled – very violently. Ned worked very, very hard and he would agree that I worked very hard as well. We don't trust each other. I think he's on an ego trip – he perhaps thought I was. I'm a lot older than he is – but I don't know. One of the other major differences between us was that Ned believed in the big event. I always believe, and believe even more, in the small movement with people who are committed. Both of us got a lot of publicity, Ned revelled in it. Last spring I asked him to come to my rooms. I shut the door and locked it from the inside and said, "Look, Ned, let's bury the hatchet and do a job together. The whole campaign needs a boost, it needs another bit of drama. I believe that we have to do an occupation. The only building worth occupying is the Information Centre because that is where all the information is, and that's what it's all about." Ned said (we even shook hands), "We'll occupy the Odhams site." Well, that's just a vacant site, so I said, "No. Do something more illegal. Ransack the files." So anyhow I finally got him to agree. This has to be split-second timing because we've got to get in there. The police were patrolling the area, much more, you see, after the campaign. I was in gaol at one time, in Bow Street, for putting up posters. The police were always watching. We'll get nine people each; nine people we can trust. Well, I believe the nine he got were no good – that's why it fell down. The nine I had were nearly all local. And what happened was we had two meetings in a room over the Opera Tavern – the landlord must have thought it was an IRA meeting – those meetings were terrific. The first time in two and a half years there was colour back in people's cheeks, there was a sparkle in their eyes. You can imagine in a campaign people got sick and tired of meetings; their time was wasted. Those two meetings were terrific. We decided to do an operation, everyone kept quiet about it. We were absolutely delighted that there was ninety-nine per cent approval of it, and that meant there was no going back to square one and talking, for instance, about what planning meant. We were going to do a job. I was going out of town, to keep out of the way. We set up special 'phone numbers . . . .

"The next thing I got was a phone call from my contact. She was crying. The building was occupied by the police. So I just put the phone down and said, "I've got to go now." The wife and kids came back and I kept calm. I have never been so angry in my life. I went past the Information Centre and sure enough it was occupied.

"I went into the community office. I must have been there for no more than thirty seconds. It was crowded – I don't know where all the people had come from but it was crowded. I have never sworn so much in my life. Every foul word I could think of. All in about thirty seconds. Ned had told a policewoman, who had said she was on our side. I left. I went into a coffee bar. Two Scottish fellows, friends of mine, came in. They were trying to calm me. That night was spent in a funny way. All those people – they would

not drink with each other. They formed naturally into their groups. I spent that night in the Cross Keys, with some local men. I was just staring into space. I suddenly realized that one of the men had vanished. An hour later he came back and his arms were covered in grease. He had just gone out to the demolition cranes with five pounds of sugar to put them out of action. He couldn't find the mechanism in the dark. That was it for me — Covent Garden. I made one more speech. I wrote a speech. I just called for the Covent Garden Freedom Movement. I said: form a new movement, the Community Association is betraying you. You see what you have now; the GLC pays for the newspaper, they pay for the posters. The planners who were fighting against us, they are still sitting across tne table, dealing with you on the Assembly meeting and the Forum meetings — the same old people . . . . Would you like another drink?"

Part of the new market at Nine Elms, Battersea

Fruit Supply Calendar

Variety	Source of Supply	In Season	Variety	Source of Supply	In Season
APPLES			Golden Delicious	Israel	Sept-Oct
Beauty of Bath	Britain	July-Aug	Belfort	Italy	Oct-Apr
Bramley	,,	All year	Golden Delicious	,,	Oct-Apr
Blenheim Orange	,,	December	Golden Russet	,,	Feb-Mar
Charles Ross	,,	October	Jonathan	,,	Oct-Apr
Cox's Orange Pippin	,,	Sept-April	Kalterer Bohmer	,,	Jan-Apr
Early Victoria ..	,,	July-Aug	Lavine	,,	Nov-Mar
Ellison Orange Pippin	,,	October	Morganduft	,,	Feb-Mar
George Cave	,,	July-Aug	Rambour Franck	,,	Nov-Feb
Grenadier	,,	July-Aug	Golden Delicious	Lebanon	Oct-Dec
James Grieve	,,	Sept-Oct	Ballarat	New Zealand	April-June
Laxton Superb	,,	Oct-Jan	Bledesloe Cox	,,	April
Lanes Prince Albert	,,	Nov-Jan	Cox's Orange Pippin	,,	April-May
Lord Derby	,,	Aug-Nov	Cleopatra	,,	June
Lord Lambourne	,,	Oct-Nov	Delicious	,,	June
Millers Seedling	,,	August	Dougherty	,,	June-July
Mutsu	,,	Aug-Sept	Dunn's Seedling	,,	April
Newton Wonder	,,	Sept-Jan	Granny Smith	,,	June-July
Russett	,,	Oct-Jan	Golden Delicious	,,	April-May
Warner	,,	Aug-Sept	Jonathan	,,	April-June
Worcesters	,,	Aug-Feb	Kidd's Orange Pippin	,,	April-May
Cleopatra	Australia	April-May	Rome Beauty	,,	July
Delicious	,,	April-June	Sturmer Pippin	,,	May-July
Cox's Orange Pippin	,,	April-May	Cox's Orange Pippin	South Africa	April
Geeveston Fancy	,,	June	Commerce	,,	April-June
Granny Smith	,,	Mar-Aug	Delicious	,,	Mar-April
Golden Delicious	,,	April	Dunn's Seedlings	,,	Mar-May
Jonathan	,,	April-June	Golden Delicious	,,	Mar-April
Rokewood	,,	July-Aug	Granny Smith	,,	April-June
Rome Beauty	,,	July	Jonathan	,,	March
Sturmer Pippin ..	,,	May-Aug	Rokewood	,,	June
Worcester Pearmain	,,	April	Rome Beauty	,,	April-June
Black Winesap	Argentina	May-June	White W.P.	,,	April-June
Black Jonathan	,,	Mar-April	Winesaps	,,	April-May
Golden Delicious	,,	Mar-May	York	,,	June
Granny Smith	,,	May-June	Golden Delicious	U.S.A	Dec-Mar
Jonathan	,,	April	McIntosh Red	,,	February
King David	,,	Mar-April	Newton Pippin	,,	Nov-Mar
Red Delicious	,,	Mar-June	Red Delicious	,,	Dec-Mar
Rome Beauty	,,	June	Winesap	,,	Jan-Mar
Jonathan	Bulgaria	December			
Golden Delicious	Canada	Nov-Feb	**APRICOTS**		
Jonathan	,,	Dec-Jan			
Newtown Pippin	,,	Feb-April		Greece	June-Aug
McIntosh Red	,,	Oct-Feb		Hungary	July-Aug
Red Delicious	,,	Feb-April		South Africa	Dec-Feb
Russet	,,	January		Spain	May-Aug
Winesap	,,	Jan-April		Turkey	June-Aug
Granny Smith	Chile	June-July			
Jonathan	,,	April	**AVOCADO PEARS**		
Cox's Orange Pippin	Denmark	Dec-Feb			
Golden Delicious	France	Sept-April		Israel	Oct-April
Cox	Germany	November		Kenya	Aug-Oct
Horneburger	,,	November		South Africa	April-Dec
Jonathans	Hungary	Oct-Jan		U.S.A	Jan-April

Variety	Source of Supply	In Season

BANANAS

Brazil	All year	
Cameroons	All year	
Canary Is.	All year	
Dominica	April-June	
Ghana	All year	
Israel	Mar-April	
Jamaica	All year	
Martinique	All year	
Windward Is.	All year	

BILBERRIES

Poland	July-Aug	

BLACKCURRANTS

Britain	June-Aug	

CHERRIES

Britain	June-Aug	
Canada	April-July	
France	May-June	
Italy	May-June	
Spain	May-June	
U.S.A	July-August	

CHINESE GOOSEBERRIES

New Zealand	July-Feb	

CLEMENTINES

Cyprus	Dec-Jan	
Spain	Dec-Jan	
Morocco	Dec-Feb	

CRANBERRIES

Holland	Jan-Feb	
U.S.A	Jan-Feb	

CUSTARD APPLES

Madeira	Sept-Feb	

DAMSONS

Britain	Aug-Oct	

DATES

Tunis	Sept-Mar	
Iraq	Oct-Dec	
Israel	Sept-Mar	

FIGS

France	Sept-Nov	

Variety	Source of Supply	In Season
	Greece	Oct-Dec
	Turkey	Nov-Dec

GRANADILLAS

	Madeira	November

GOOSEBERRIES

	Hungary	June

GRAPES

Colmar	Britain	Nov-Dec
Muscat	,,	Nov-Dec
Alicante	Belgium	June-Aug
Colmar	,,	Oct-Feb
Muscat	,,	Nov-Dec
Royal	,,	June-Aug
	,,	November
Almeria	Chile	May
Red Emperor	,,	May
Rozaki	Cyprus	Aug-Sept
Seedless	,,	July-Aug
Sultanas	,,	July-Aug
Alphonse Lavalle	France	Aug-Oct
	Greece	Sept-Oct
Alicante	Holland	July-Feb
Alphonse	Israel	July-Aug
Perlette	,,	June-July
Sultana	,,	June-July
Waltham Cross	,,	July
	Italy	July-Nov
	Morocco	December
Sweet Water	Portugal	July-Oct
Almeria	South Africa	May-June
Alphonse Lavalle	,,	Feb-Mar
Barlinka	,,	Mar-June
Colmar	,,	Mar-April
Golden Hill	,,	Mar-May
New Cross	,,	Mar-May
Olivette	,,	Feb-Mar
Prune-de-Cazoul	,,	Mar-April
Waltham Cross	,,	Feb-April
Queen of the Vineyard	,,	February
Almeria	Spain	Oct-Jan
	Turkey	September
Red Emperor	U.S.A	Oct-Jan

GRAPEFRUIT

	Brazil	April-Aug
	British	
	Honduras	Sept-Oct
	Cuba	Sept-Nov
	Cyprus	Dec-April
	Israel	Nov-May
	Jamaica	June-Oct
	Morocco	Jan-May

Variety	Source of Supply	In Season
	Paraguay	April-July
	South Africa	April-Oct
	Spain	Oct-Nov
	Surinam	Sept-Nov
	Trinidad	Oct-April
	U.S.A	June-Aug

GREENGAGES

	Britain	July-Aug
	Italy	July
	Spain	June-Aug

KUMQUATS

	Morocco	Feb-April

LEMONS

	Cyprus	Aug-April
	Greece	Oct-Dec
	Israel	Mar-June
	Italy	All year
	Morocco	Nov-Dec
	Spain	Oct-Nov
	S. Africa	All year
	U.S.A	June-Aug

LIMES

	South Africa	July-Sept
	West Indies	Oct-Aug

LITCHES

	South Africa	Dec-Feb

LOGANBERRIES

	Britain	July-Aug

MANDARINS

	Italy	Dec-Mar
	Morocco	Oct-Jan
	Spain	Nov-Feb

MANGOES

	India	May-July
	Kenya	Jan-Sept

MEDLARS

	Britain	November

MELONS

Barglo (Green)	Argentina	Feb-June
Ogen	Canary	June-Aug
Black Tendral	Chile	Feb-June
Honeydew	,,	Feb-June

Variety	Source of Supply	In Season
White	,,	Feb-June
Water	Cyprus	July
Charentais	France	June-Sept
Net	Holland	July-Sept
Tiger	,,	July-Sept
Ogen	Israel	May-Sept
Water	,,	June-Aug
Yellow	,,	June-July
Green	Morocco	October
Yellow	,,	Aug-Nov
White	South Africa	Dec-May
Charentais	Spain	Mar-Sept
White		Aug-Nov
Charentais		Mar-Sept
Green Honeydew	,,	July-Dec
Ogen	,,	July-Sept
Water	,,	Aug-Sept
Yellow	,,	Aug-Oct

NECTARINES

	Britain	July-Aug
	Belgium	May
	South Africa	Dec-Mar
	U.S.A.	Aug-Sept

ORANGES

Navels	Australia	April-May
Navels	Brazil	April-Dec
Ovals	Cyprus	Dec-April
Valencia Lates	,,	Mar-April
Jaffa Shamoutis	Israel	Dec-April
Valencia Lates	,,	April-May
Palermo Bitters	Italy	Jan-Feb
Cadeneras	Morocco	Feb-April
Hamlins	,,	January
Navels	,,	Jan-May
Valencia Lates	,,	Mar-June
Hamlins	South Africa	June
Letaba Early	,,	July-Aug
Mediterranean Sweet	,,	July-Sept
Mid-Season	,,	June-Sept
Navels	,,	May-Nov
Seedling	,,	Aug-Sept
Valencia Lates	,,	Aug-Nov
Blancas	Spain	Jan-Feb
Bloods	,,	Feb-Mar
Cadeneras	,,	Jan-Mar
Navels	,,	Oct-Feb
Seville Bitters	,,	Dec-Feb
Valencia Lates	,,	April-May
Vernas	,,	April-May
Maltaise	Tunisia	Jan-April
Californian	U.S.A	Feb-Sept

ORTANIQUES

	Jamaica	Jan-April

Variety	Source of Supply	In Season
	PASSION FRUIT	
	Kenya	Feb-Mar
	Madeira	January
	PEACHES	
Glasshouse	Britain	June-Aug
Outdoor	Canada	October
	France	June-Aug
	Greece	September
Amsden	Italy, Spain	June-Sept
Cardinal	,,	,,
Dixie Red	,,	,,
Fairhaven	,,	,,
Hales	,,	,,
Mayflower	,,	,,
Southland	,,	,,
Culemborg	South Africa	Dec-Jan
Duke of York	,,	January
Early Dawn	,,	Dec-Jan
Inkoos	,,	Dec-Jan
Marina	,,	Jan-Feb
Peregrine	,,	Jan-Feb
Pucelle	,,	Feb-Mar
Rhodes	,,	Dec-Feb
Van Riebeeck	,,	January
	Spain	June-July
Hales	Turkey	Aug-Oct
	U.S.A	April
	PEARS	
Beurre Hardy	Britain	Sept-Dec
Clapps	,,	Aug-Sept
Comice	,,	Oct-Dec
Conference	,,	Sept-Feb
Dr. Jules	,,	Aug-Sept
Fertility	,,	October
Packhams Triumph	,,	November
Williams	,,	Sept-Dec
Winter Nelis	,,	Nov-Jan
Anjou	Argentina	Mar-April
Beurre Hardy	,,	March
Williams	,,	Feb-Mar
Winter Nelis	,,	Feb-Mar
Anjou	Australia	May-June
Beurre Bosc	,,	May-July
Comice	,,	May-June
Josephine	,,	April-July
Packham's Triumph	,,	April-June
Williams	,,	April
Winter Cole	,,	May-July
Winter Nelis	,,	July
Beurre Hardy	Holland	Nov-Feb
Conference	,,	Nov-Feb
Williams	Italy	July-Oct
Beurre Bosc	New Zealand	April-June
Packhams	,,	April-May
Louise Bonne	,,	April-May

Variety	Source of Supply	In Season
Williams	,,	Mar-April
Winter Cole	,,	April-May
Winter Nelis	,,	May-June
Bon Cretien	South Africa	Feb-Mar
Beurre Bosc	,,	Feb-April
Beurre Hardy	,,	Feb-April
Clapp's Favourite	,,	Jan-Feb
Comice	,,	Mar-April
Glou Morceau	,,	April-May
Josephine	,,	Mar-May
Keiffer	,,	Mar-June
Louise Bonne	,,	Feb-April
Packham's Triumph	,,	Feb-May
Winter Neils	,,	April-June
Guyot	Spain	July-Aug
Limoneras	,,	
	PINEAPPLES	
St. Michael's	Azores	All year
Red Spanish	Jamaica	June-Sept
	Kenya	All year
	Martinique	Oct-Jan
Cayenne	South Africa	Nov-July
Queen	,,	All year
	PLUMS	
Belles de Louvain	Britain	August
Bush	,,	Aug-Sept
Czars	,,	June-Aug
Droopers	,,	September
Monarch	,,	Sept-Oct
Oullins Gage	,, Aug	July-Aug
Pershore	,,	August
Pond's	,,	Aug-Sept
Switchen	,,	Sept-Oct
Victoria	,,	Aug-Sept
President	Argentina	April-May
Switchen	Bulgaria	Aug-Oct
	Hungary	Aug-Oct
Florentia	Italy	June-July
Gaviota	,,	July
Gaviota	,,	July
Santa Rosa	,,	June-July
Switzen	Yugoslavia	Aug-Sept
Beauty	South-Africa	Dec-Jan
Gaviota	,,	Jan-Mar
Golden King	,,	Feb-April
Kelsey	,,	Feb-Mar
President	,,	March
Santa Rosa	,,	Dec-Feb
Formosa	Spain	July
Santa Rosa	,,	July
Santa Rosa	U.S.A	Sept-Oct
	POMEGRANATES	
Cyprus		Oct-Nov

Variety	*Source of Supply*	*In Season*
	Israel	Sept-Nov
	Spain	Oct-Nov

RASPBERRIES

	Britain	June-Sept
	France	May-June

REDCURRANTS

	Britain	June-Aug

RHUBARB

Forced	Britain	Dec-Mar
Outdoor	,,	Mar-June

SATSUMAS

	Spain	Oct-Dec

STRAWBERRIES

Cloche	Britain	April-June
Hothouse	,,	Jan-April
Outdoor	,,	May-October
	Cyprus	April-May
	France	April-June
	Greece	April-May
	Guernsey	May
	Holland	April-May
	Israel	January
	Jersey	June
	Kenya	Sept-May
	New Zealand	Dec-Mar
	Spain	Feb-April
	U.S.A	Mar-May

TOMATOES

	Britain	April-Oct
	Bulgaria	Mar-April
	Canary Is.	Oct-May
	Guernsey	Mar-Oct
	Holland	Mar-Oct
	Israel	Dec-Feb
	Jersey	April-Oct
	Malta	Jan-April
	Spain	Oct-Feb

Vegetable Supply Calendar

Variety	Source of Supply	In Season
ARTICHOKES		
Globe	Britain	June-Sept
Globe	France	March-Nov
Globe	Italian	Aug-Oct
Globe	Spain	Dec-June
Jerusalem	Home	March-July
ASPARAGUS		
	Britain	May-July
	Cape	Sept-Jan
	France	Feb-May
	Israel	March-May
	Kenya	Feb-April
	Tunis	March-May
	U.S.A.	Jan-April
AUBERGINES		
	Canary Islands	Jan-June
	Israel	Oct-March
	France	March-Nov
	Spain	May-Aug
	Italy	June-Sept
BATAVIA		
	Spain	Dec-Jan
BEANS		
Hot-house	Britain	March-Aug
Runner	Britain	July-Oct
Broad	Britain	June-July
Forced	France	Nov-July
String	Kenya	Dec-May
String	Canary Islands	March
Broad	France	April-May
Broad	Italy	April
String	France	May-June
String	Spain	May-June
Broad	Spain	May
Bobi	Italy	June-July
Hot-house	Guernsey	March-Aug
Outdoor	Britain	June-Sept
French	Italy	
Broad	France	May-June
BEETROOT		
	Britain	All year
	Italy	May-July

Variety	Source of Supply	In Season
BRUSSELS SPROUTS		
	Britain	Aug-April
CABBAGE		
January King	Britain	Oct-April
Drumhead	Britain	Aug-Nov
Spring Green	Britain	Nov-March
Primo	Britain	June-Mid Aug
Red	Britain	Dec-Feb
White	Holland	Sept-June
Red	Holland	Sept-June
CAPSICUMS		
Canary Islands	April-Aug	
		Dec
Cyprus	June	
Egypt		
France	June-Dec	
Israel	Dec-June	
Italy	July-Oct	
Kenya	Feb-June	
CARROTS		
	Britain	All year (break May-June)
	Algeria	April-May
	Canada	April-June
	Cyprus	March-June
	France	April-June
	Holland	All year
	Italy	Feb-July
	U.S.A.	April-July
CAULIFLOWER/BROCCOLI		
	Britain	All year Broc
	Jersey	Nov-Feb
	France	Nov-April
	Holland	June
	Italy	Nov-March
CELERIAC		
	Britain	Sept-March
	France	Sept-Dec
CELERY		
	Britain	June-Feb
	U.S.A.	Jan-July
	Israel	March-June

Variety	Source of Supply	In Season
	CHICORY	
(Witloof)	Belgium	Sept-June
	CHILLIES	
	Canary Islands	March-July
	France	June-Feb
	Kenya	July
	CORN-on-the-COB	
	Britain	Aug-Oct
	France	July-Aug
	Italy	July-Aug
	U.S.A.	Aug-Sept
	COURGETTES	
	Britain	June-Sept
	France	May-June
	Canary Islands	January
	France	Oct-June
	Jersey	June-July
	Ethiopia	June-July
	East Africa	June-July
	CUCUMBER	
	Britain	March-Oct
	Canary Islands	Nov-March
	Holland	March-Dec
	ENDIVE	
	Britain	May-Aug
	France	Sept-May
	Italy	February
	Spain	Jan-March
	FENNEL	
	France	Oct-Jan
	Italy	June-March
	GARLIC	
	France	All year
	Italy	Aug-March
	Portugal	Feb-March
	LEEKS	
	Britain & Ireland	Aug-April
	LETTUCE	
	Britain, Indoor	

Variety	Source of Supply	In Season
	& Out	All year
	France	Dec-April
	Holland	Oct-June
	Italy	Feb-April
	Jersey	May-Aug
	Spain	Feb-May
Cos	Israel	Oct-April
	MARROWS	
	Britain	June-Oct
	MINT	
Indoor	Britain	Oct-Jan
	MUSHROOMS	
	Britain	All year
	MUSTARD and CRESS	
		All year
	OCRA	
	Cyprus	
	Kenya	June-Sept
	Morocco	
	ONIONS	
	Britain	Sept-Jan
	Canada	Aug-April
	Canary Islands	May-April
	Cape	March-May
	Chile	Feb-July
	Egypt	March-July
	Holland	July-May
	Hungary	Aug-Feb
	Israel	July-Nov
	Italy	Sept-Feb
	Poland	Oct-March
	Spain	All year
	U.S.A.	Nov-May
	PARSLEY	
	Britain	April-Jan
	France	Jan-May
	Jersey	Nov-Feb
	PARSNIPS	
	Britain	Sept-April

Variety	Source of Supply	In Season		Variety	Source of Supply	In Season
	PEAS				**TURNIPS**	
	Britain	May-Oct			Britain	All year (April-June break)
	POTATOES				France	April-June
Ware	Britain	August on			**WATERCRESS**	
New	Britain	June-July			Britain	All year
New	Belgium	May-June				
New	Canary Islands	Nov-June				
Ware	Cyprus	Dec-Jan				
New	Cyprus	March-June				
New	Egypt	May-June				
New	Greece	May-June				
New	France	June				
New	Guernsey	Jan-April				
New	Israel	March-May				
New	Italy	Nov-June				
New	Italy	May-June				
New	Jersey	May-July				
New	Malta	April-Aug				
New	Morocco	Dec-May				
New	Spain	April-June				

Variety	Source of Supply	In Season
	PUMPKIN	
	Britain	Aug-Oct
	Italy	June-July
	RADISH	
	Britain	April-Oct
Glasshouse	Guernsey	Dec-May
	Holland	March
	SALSIFY	
	Belgium	Oct-June
	France	Oct
	SEAKALE	
	Britain	Dec-March
	SPINACH	
	Britain	April-Nov
	France	Nov-Apr
	SWEDES	
	Britain	Sept-May
	SWEET POTATOES	
	Canary Islands	Sept-June

BIBLIOGRAPHY

Beck, Betholle, Child: *Mastering the Art of French Cooking* (Cassell, 1963).
Walter G. Bell: *The Great Fire of London* (1920).
Walter G. Bell: *The Great Plague in London* (1924).
Mary Cathcart Borer: *Covent Garden* (Abelard-Schuman, 1967).
Marcel Boulestin: *A Second Helping* (Heinemann, 1928).
R. Bradley: *The Country Housewife and Lady's Director in the Management of the House, and the Delights and Profits of a Farm* (Woodman & Lyon, Covent Garden, 1727).
N.G. Brett-James: *The Growth of Stuart London* (1935).
May Byron: *Pot Luck* (Hodder & Stoughton, 1913).
Cadwaller and Ohr: *The Whole Earth Cookbook* (Andre Deutsch, 1973).
Peter Cunningham: *Inigo Jones — A Life of the Architect* (Shakespeare Society, 1848).
Elizabeth David: *French Provincial Cooking* (Michael Joseph, 1960).
Alan Dent: *My Covent Garden* (Dent).
John Farley: *The London Art of Cookery and Housekeepers Complete Assistant on a New Plan* (1783).
Gerardes Herballe (1633).
R. Jacobs: *Covent Garden, its Romance and History* (Simpkin, Marshall, Hamilton, Kent, 1913).
Marie de Joncourt: *Wholesome Cookery* (Kegan Paul, Trench, Trubner, 1895).
Col. A.R. Kenney-Herbert: *Vegetarian and Simple Diet* (Swan, Sonnen, Scheim, 1907).
H.L. Sidney Lear: *Maigre Cookery* (1884).
J. Lees-Milne: *The Age of Inigo Jones* (Batsford, 1953).
M.L. Lemery: *A Treatise of all Sorts of Foods, both Animal and Vegetable, also of Drinkables* (1745).
Sir Harry Luke: *The Tenth Muse* (1962).
Will Rabisha: *The Whole Body of Cookery Dissected* (1661).
Craig Sams: *About Macrobiotics* (Thorsons, 1972).
R. Webber: *Mud Salad Market* (Dent, 1969).
Florence White: *Flowers as Food* (Cape, 1934).

INDEX